초등 영어 교재의 베스트셀러

초등 영어 문법 실력 쌓기!

Grammar Builder

2

Grammar Builder 2

ⓒ2015 by I am Books

지은이	이상건
펴낸이	신성현, 오상욱
기획 · 편집	이두희
영업관리	장신동, 허윤정
펴낸곳	도서출판 아이엠북스
	153-802 서울시 금천구 가산동 327-32 대륭테크노타운 12차 1116호
대표전화	02-6343-0999
팩스	02-6343-0995
출판등록	2006년 6월 7일
	제 313-2006-000122호
ISBN	978-89-6398-098-0 63740

www.iambooks.co.kr

초등 영어 교재의 베스트셀러

초등 영어 문법 실력 쌓기!

Grammar Builder 2

You Are the Only One!

Words in Grammar

I am books

street	거리	Many people walk on the street.	많은 사람들이 거리를 걷는다.
laptop	노트북	Dan carries his laptop.	Dan은 그의 노트북을 운반한다.
finish	끝내다	The boy finishes his homework.	그 소년은 그의 숙제를 마친다.
exam	시험	They pass the exam.	그들은 그 시험을 통과한다.
wear	입다, 쓰다	Steve wears a cap.	Steve는 모자를 쓴다.
work	일하다, 작동하다	It works well.	그것은 잘 작동한다.
respect	존경하다	They respect her.	그들은 그녀를 존경한다.
prove	증명하다	The scientists prove that.	그 과학자들은 저것을 증명한다.
miss	놓치다, 그리워하다	She misses the bus.	그녀는 그 버스를 놓친다.
slip	미끄러지다	I slip and fall down on the ice.	나는 미끄러져 얼음 위에 넘어진다.
trip	여행	Jessica takes a long trip.	Jessica는 긴 여행을 한다.
actor	배우	He wants to be an actor.	그는 배우가 되기를 원한다.
post office	우체국	They work at the post office.	그들은 우체국에서 일한다.
lawyer	변호사	His daughter wants to be a lawyer.	그의 딸은 변호사가 되기를 원한다.
subway	지하철	Mia goes to her work by subway.	Mia는 지하철로 그녀의 회사에 간다.
hurry	서두르다	She hurries up in the morning.	그녀는 아침에 서두른다.
cross	건너다	Susan crosses the street.	Susan은 거리를 건넌다.
end	끝나다	The concert ends at 2 o'clock.	그 콘서트는 정각 2시에 끝난다.
fix	고치다	My father fixes the computer.	나의 아버지는 그 컴퓨터를 고친다.
pass	건네주다	He passes me the salt.	그는 나에게 소금을 건네준다.
delicious	맛있는	They enjoy delicious food.	그들은 맛있는 음식을 즐긴다.
brush	빗질하다	We brush the kid's hair everyday.	우리는 그 아이의 머리를 매일 빗질한다.
something	뭔가	The babies eat something all day.	그 아기들은 온종일 뭔가를 먹는다.
mosquito	모기	They catch five mosquitoes.	그들은 모기 5마리를 잡는다.
classical	고전의	She watches classical movies.	그녀는 고전 영화를 좋아한다.
wood	목재	The truck carries wood.	그 트럭은 목재를 나른다.
hug	껴안다	They hugs and say good-bye.	그들은 껴안고 작별인사를 한다.
repeat	반복하다	The children repeats the words.	그 아이들은 그 말들을 반복한다.
copy	따라하다, 복제하다	My brother always copy me.	나의 남동생은 항상 나를 따라한다.
yoga	요가	They do yoga everyday.	그들은 매일 요가를 한다.

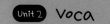

onion	양파	I don't like onions.	나는 양파를 좋아하지 않는다.
early	일찍	We don't get up early.	우리는 일찍 일어나지 않는다.
pay	지불하다, 돈을 내다	Do the men pay every time?	그 남자들은 매번 지불하니?
gate	문, 출입문	Does she stand at the gate?	그녀는 문에 서 있니?
apartment	아파트	Olivia lives in an apartment.	Olivia는 아파트에서 산다.
luggage	짐	Ann carries the heavy luggage.	Ann은 그 무거운 짐을 운반한다.
belong	속하다	It belongs to Bill.	그것은 Bill의 것이다.
chat	수다 떨다	They chats with their friends.	그들은 그들의 친구들과 수다를 떤다.
guest	손님	Tony welcomes the guests.	Tony는 그 손님들을 맞이한다.
remember	기억하다	I don't remember his address.	나는 그의 주소를 기억하지 못한다.
chew	씹다	She doesn't chew gum in class.	그녀는 수업 중에 껌을 씹지 않는다.
exercise	운동하다	Do you exercise every day?	너는 매일 운동하니?
truth	사실, 진실	Do you tell the truth?	너는 진실을 말하니?
noise	소음	Do I make noise?	내가 소음을 만드나요?
bark	짖다	Do the dogs bark a lot?	그 개들은 많이 짖니?
address	주소	You know his address.	너는 그의 주소를 안다.
grocery	식료품	Does he buy groceries here?	그는 여기서 식료품을 사니?
receive	받다	I receive his e-mail.	나는 그에게 이메일을 받는다.
lesson	수업, 레슨	I take a piano lesson every day.	나는 매일 피아노 수업을 듣는다.
alone	혼자	Cindy stays home alone.	Cindy는 혼자 집에 머무른다.
shower	샤워	The man takes a shower.	그 남자는 샤워를 한다.
voice	목소리	You hear my voice.	너는 나의 목소리를 듣는다.
airport	공항	Ava arrives at the airport.	Ava는 공항에 도착한다.
meal	식사	You do the dishes after meals.	너는 식사 후에 설거지를 한다.
cook	요리사	Mr. Baker is a cook.	Baker 씨는 요리사이다.
well	건강한	Your grandfather looks well.	너의 할아버지는 건강해 보이신다.
diary	일기	He keeps a diary every day.	그는 매일 일기를 쓴다.
enter	들어가다	He doesn't enter the house.	그는 그 집에 들어가지 않는다.
health	건강	Do you worry about the health?	너는 건강에 대해 걱정하니?
ring	울리다	The woman doesn't ring the bell.	그 여자는 그 벨을 울리지 않는다.

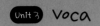
clerk	점원	There are four clerks in the store.	그 상점에는 4명의 점원이 있다.
between	~ 사이에	There is a printer between the computers.	그 컴퓨터 사이에 프린터기가 있다.
oven	오븐	There is an oven in the dining room.	식당에는 오븐이 있다.
pillow	베개	There is four pillows on the bed.	그 침대에는 베개 4개가 있다.
refrigerator	냉장고	There is food in the refrigerator.	냉장고에는 음식이 있다.
among	~ 사이에	There is bees among the flowers.	그 꽃들 사이에 벌들이 있다.
garden	정원	There are flowers in the garden.	그 정원에는 꽃들이 있다.
plate	접시	There is little food on the plate.	접시에는 음식이 거의 없다.
pocket	주머니	There are four coins in my pocket.	나의 주머니에는 동전 4개가 있다.
island	섬	It takes an hour to Jeju island by plane.	비행기로 제주도까지 1시간 걸린다.
beside	옆에	There is a man beside the woman.	그 여자 옆에 한 남자가 있다.
lamp	전등, 램프	Turn on the lamp.	전등을 켜라.
kitten	새끼 고양이	There is a kitten around my house.	나의 집 주위에 새끼 고양이 1마리가 9
hole	구멍	There is an ant near the hole.	그 구멍 근처에 개미가 있다.
tulip	튤립	There is a butterfly among the tulips.	그 튤립들 사이에 나비가 있다.
storage	창고	There is a lot of rice in the storage.	그 창고에 많은 쌀이 있다.
pet shop	애완동물 가게	There are puppies in the pet shop.	애완동물 가게에 강아지들이 있다.
university	대학	Are there many universities in Japan?	일본에는 많은 대학들이 있니?
bill	지폐	There are five bills in my purse.	나의 지갑에는 지폐 5장이 있다.
country	시골, 나라	My house is in the country.	나의 집은 시골에 있다.
basket	바구니	There are two loaves of bread in the basket.	그 바구니에는 빵 2덩어리가 있다.
plastic	플라스틱	There is little rice in the plastic bag.	그 플라스틱 가방에는 쌀이 거의 없다.
foreign	외국인의	There are foreign teachers here.	여기에는 외국인 선생님들이 있다.
behind	~ 뒤에	A bank is behind the building.	은행은 그 건물 뒤에 있다.
cage	우리	A fox is in the cage.	여우는 그 우리 안에 있다.
bottle	병	Five bottles of juice are on the shelf.	주스 5병은 선반 위에 있다.
gym	체육관	There is one man in the gym.	체육관에 남자 1명이 있다.
furniture	가구	There are six pieces of furniture in the room.	방에는 가구 6점이 있다.
plants	식물	There is many plants at the flower shop.	꽃가게에는 많은 식물들이 있다.
season	계절	There is four seasons in Korea.	한국에는 4계절이 있다.

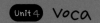

handsome	잘생긴	The man is very handsome.	그 남자는 매우 잘 생겼다.
cool	멋진, 시원한	It is very cool game.	그것은 매우 멋진 게임이다.
famous	유명한	She has famous pictures.	그녀는 유명한 그림들을 가지고 있다.
outside	바깥쪽	It is windy outside.	바깥에 바람이 분다.
bring	가져오다	He brings us happy news.	그는 우리에게 행복한 소식을 가져다준다.
coat	코트	It is a very long coat.	그것은 매우 긴 코트이다.
fall	떨어지다	The leaves are falling.	그 나뭇잎들은 떨어지고 있다.
painting	그림	I love her beautiful paintings.	나는 그녀의 아름다운 그림들을 사랑한다.
smart	영리한	John is his smart son.	John의 그의 영리한 아들이다.
useful	유용한	Those are very useful books.	저것들은 매우 유용한 책들이다.
diligent	부지런한	That diligent woman is my friend.	저 부지런한 여자는 나의 친구이다.
lazy	게으른	Her sister is lazy.	그녀의 여동생은 게으르다.
sneakers	운동화	His sneakers are dirty.	그의 운동화는 더럽다.
deep	깊은	The river is deep.	그 강은 깊다.
ring	반지	The ring is expensive.	그 반지는 비싸다.
volleyball	배구	The volleyball players are tall.	그 배구 선수들은 키가 크다.
narrow	좁은	The road is narrow.	그 길은 좁다.
wide	넓은	The road is not wide.	그 길은 넓지 않다.
light	가벼운, 밝은	The furniture is not light.	그 가구는 가볍지 않다.
unkind	불친절한	The doctor is not unkind.	그 의사는 불친절하지 않다.
safe	안전한	The street is not safe.	그 거리는 안전하지 않다.
thin	마른	My mother is thin and tall.	나의 어머니는 마르고 키가 크다.
swimming suit	수영복	This swimming suit is wet.	이 수영복은 젖어 있다.
interesting	재미있는	These books are very interesting.	이 책들은 매우 재미있다.
watch	손목시계	This watch is very expensive.	이 손목시계는 매우 비싸다.
roof	지붕	The roofs are green.	그 지붕들은 초록색이다.
excellent	훌륭한	She is very an excellent cook.	그녀는 매우 훌륭한 요리사이다.
cheap	싼	This is a cheap house.	이것은 싼 집이다.
place	장소	These are beautiful places.	이것들은 아름다운 장소들이다.
cookie	쿠키	These are sweet cookies.	이것들은 달콤한 쿠키들이다.

sound	소리	I don't hear any sounds there.	나는 거기서 어떤 소리도 들을 수 없다
question	질문	The girl asks some questions.	그 소녀는 약간의 질문을 한다.
comic book	만화책	I don't have any comic books.	나는 약간의 만화책이 없다.
fork	포크	Do you need any forks?	너는 약간의 포크가 필요하니?
information	정보	She can't get any information.	그녀는 어떤 정보도 얻을 수가 없다.
holiday	휴일	The store closes every holiday.	그 가게는 모든 공휴일에 문을 닫는다.
break	쉬는 시간	All the girls chat during the break.	모든 소녀들은 쉬는 시간 동안 수다를 떤다.
attention	집중	Every one, attention please!	모두들, 집중해주세요!
beach	해변	He goes to the beach every summer.	그는 매 여름마다 해변에 간다.
person	사람	Every person needs love.	모든 사람들은 사람을 필요로 한다.
future	미래, 장래	Every man has future plans.	모든 사람은 장래 계획을 가지고 있다.
true	진정한	Every girl wants true friends.	모든 소녀는 진정한 친구들을 원한다.
classmate	급우	She meets some classmates.	그녀는 몇몇 학우를 만난다.
picnic	소풍	Every spring, we go on a picnic.	매 봄마다 우리는 소풍을 간다.
quiet	조용한	All giraffes are very quiet.	모든 기린들은 매우 조용하다.
fresh	신선한	They don't have fresh milk.	그들은 신선한 우유가 없다.
cut	자르다	Does he cut tall trees?	그는 큰 나무를 자르니?
raise	기르다	Joe raises some pets.	Joe는 몇몇 애완동물을 기른다.
poem	시	He writes some poems.	그는 약간의 시를 쓴다.
collect	수집하다	She collects some foreign coins.	그녀는 약간의 외국의 동전을 모은다.
ticket	티켓	There aren't any tickets here.	여기에는 티켓이 없습니다.
close	가까운, 친한	I have some close friends.	나는 몇몇 친한 친구들이 있다.
borrow	빌리다	Does Suji borrow any books?	수지는 약간의 책들을 빌리니?
surprising	놀라운	We have surprising news.	우리는 놀라운 소식을 가지고 있다.
pour	쏟다	She pours some flours in the bowl.	그녀는 그 그릇에 약간의 밀가루를 쏟는다.
poison	독	Do all snakes have poison?	모든 뱀들은 독을 가지고 있니?
locked	잠긴	Every door is closed and locked.	모든 문은 닫혀있고 잠겨 있다.
teenager	십대	All teenagers are good at singer.	모든 10대들은 노래를 잘한다.
search	찾다	He searches information about the accident.	그는 그 사고에 대한 정보를 찾는다.
come true	이루어지다	Every hope comes true.	모든 희망은 이루어진다.

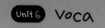
travel	여행하다	The man travels many countries.	그 남자는 많은 나라들을 여행한다.
forest	숲	There aren't many deer in the forest.	그 숲에는 많은 사슴들이 없다.
hive	벌집	There are many bees in the hive.	벌집에는 많은 벌들이 있다.
accessory	액세서리	She wears many accessories.	그녀는 많은 액세서리를 걸친다.
spend	소비하다	He spends a lot of money for shopping.	그는 쇼핑에 많은 돈을 소비한다.
desert	사막	He find a lot of oil in the desert.	그는 사막에서 많은 오일을 발견한다.
pain	통증	The driver feels a lot of pain.	그 운전자는 많은 고통을 느낀다.
snack	간식	Do you eat much snack?	너는 많은 간식을 먹니?
space	공간	The laptops need a little space.	그 노트북들은 약간의 공간이 필요하다.
writer	작가	The writer visits few countries.	그 작가는 나라들을 거의 방문하지 않는다.
idea	생각, 아이디어	I have a few ideas.	나는 몇몇 생각들이 있다.
shampoo	샴푸	I use little shampoo.	나는 샴푸를 거의 사용하지 않는다.
cure	치료하다	The doctor cures a few sick people.	그 의사는 몇몇 아픈 사람들을 치료한다.
help	도움	The boy needs little help.	그 소년은 도움이 거의 필요 없다.
different	다른	He can speak different languages.	그는 다른 언어들을 말할 수 있다.
color	색깔	There are few colors in this painting.	이 그림에는 색깔이 거의 없다.
bake	굽다	My mom doesn't bake much bread.	나의 엄마는 많은 빵을 굽지 않는다.
mistake	실수	I make many mistakes.	나는 많은 실수를 한다.
gas	가스	We don't have a lot of gas.	우리는 많은 가스가 없다.
luck	행운, 운	I need a lot of luck.	나는 많은 행운이 필요하다.
oxygen	산소	There is little oxygen in this tank.	이 탱크 안에 산소가 거의 없다.
honey	꿀	The cook uses a little honey.	그 요리사는 약간의 꿀을 사용한다.
yogurt	요구르트	The kid eats a little yogurt.	그 아이는 약간의 요구르트를 먹는다.
mailbox	우편함	There are few letters in the mailbox.	우편함에 편지가 거의 없다.
hit	치다	The player hits many balls.	그 선수는 많은 공들을 친다.
prepare	준비하다	I don't have much time for preparing the exam.	나는 시험 준비할 시간이 많지 않다.
pond	연못	Many fish are in the pond.	많은 물고기들이 연못에 있다.
pitcher	투수	The pitcher catches many balls.	그 투수는 많은 공들을 잡는다.
closet	옷장	Judy has many clothes in the closet.	Judy는 옷장에 많은 옷들이 있다.
yard	마당	There are a few dogs in the yard.	마당에 개 몇 마리가 있다.

answer	대답하다	The clerk answers kindly.	그 점원은 친절하게 대답한다.
fatty	기름진	Fatty food is dangerous.	기름진 음식은 위험하다.
athlete	운동선수	They are very good athletes.	그들은 매우 훌륭한 운동선수이다.
pitch	던지다	The pitcher pitches perfectly.	그 투수는 완벽하게 던진다.
flood	홍수	Flood is very dangerous.	홍수는 매우 위험하다.
loudly	시끄럽게	The dog barks loudly.	그 개는 시끄럽게 짖는다.
tunnel	터널	He passes through the tunnel slowly.	그는 천천히 터널을 통과하여 지나간다.
ready	준비된	You are rarely ready for class.	너는 수업 준비가 거의 안 되었다.
backpack	배낭	His backpack is always heavy.	그의 배낭은 항상 무겁다.
kindness	친절	I can never forget his kindness.	나는 결코 그의 친절을 잊을 수 없다.
act	행동하다	You should listen carefully and act.	너는 주의 깊게 듣고, 행동해야 한다.
turtle	거북	Turtles move very slowly.	거북들은 매우 천천히 움직인다.
suddenly	갑자기	Suddenly the horse falls down.	갑자기 그 말이 넘어진다.
lake	호수	We swim in the lake.	우리는 호수에서 수영한다.
reporter	기자	The reporter is very busy.	그 기자는 매우 바쁘다.
hair style	머리 모양	I change my hair style.	나는 나의 머리 모양을 바꾼다.
credit card	신용카드	He uses his credit card.	그는 그의 신용카드를 사용한다.
frozen	언	The river is frozen in winter.	그 강은 겨울에 언다.
designer	디자이너	The designer makes a dress.	그 디자이너는 드레스를 만든다.
coach	코치	The coach talks to the players.	그 코치는 그 선수들에게 말한다.
dolphin	돌고래	The dolphin jumps high.	그 돌고래는 높이 뛰어오른다.
brush	닦다	I brush my teeth carefully.	나는 주의해서 양치질을 한다.
comfortable	편안한	The sofa is really comfortable.	그 소파는 정말 편안하다.
pianist	피아니스트	The pianist plays the piano.	그 피아니스트는 피아노를 연주한다.
fried	튀긴	She often cooks a fried chicken.	그녀는 가끔 튀긴 닭을 요리한다.
history	역사	He teaches history very easily.	그는 매우 쉽게 역사를 가르친다.
foolish	어리석은	Men are sometimes foolish.	남자들은 때때로 어리석다.
wig	가발	She always wears a wig.	그녀는 항상 가발을 쓴다.
walk	산책	I often take a walk in the evening.	나는 저녁에 종종 산책을 한다.
spaghetti	스파게티	She sometimes cooks spaghetti.	그녀는 때때로 스파게티를 요리한다.

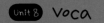

past	과거	She is lying about her past.	그녀는 그녀의 과거에 대해 거짓말을 하고 있다.
die	죽다	The fish are dying under the river.	그 물고기는 강 아래서 죽고 있다.
boots	부츠	She is wearing boots now.	그녀는 지금 부츠를 신고 있다.
twice	두 번	My mom swims twice a week.	나의 엄마는 일주일에 두 번 수영한다.
around	주변	They are running at the playground.	그들은 운동장에서 달리고 있다.
cell phone	휴대폰	She is using her cell phone.	그녀는 그녀의 휴대폰을 사용한다.
speech	연설	My father is beginning his speech.	나의 아버지는 그의 연설을 시작하고 있다.
knock	노크하다	A man is knocking on the door.	한 남자가 문을 노크하고 있다.
someone	누군가	He hears someone's voice.	그는 누군가의 목소리를 듣는다.
climb	오르다	My brother is climbing the mountain.	나의 형은 그 산을 오르고 있다.
front	앞	I am using the front door.	나는 앞문을 사용하고 있다.
mind	마음	Dan understands her mind.	Dan은 그녀의 마음을 이해한다.
accident	사건	Joshua lies about the accident.	Joshua는 그 사건에 대해 거짓말한다.
knit	뜨개질하다	They knit a scarf.	그들은 목도리를 뜨개질한다.
road	길	They aren't crossing the road.	그들은 그 길을 건너가고 있지 않다.
lie	눕다, 거짓말하다	Mike isn't lying on the sand.	Mike는 모래 위에 눕고 있지 않다.
feed	먹이를 주다	John is feeding his cat.	John은 그의 고양이에게 먹이를 주고 있다.
machine	기계	They are using this new machine.	그들은 이 새로운 기계를 사용하고 있다.
jump rope	줄넘기하다	They aren't jumping rope.	그들은 줄넘기를 하고 있지 않다.
set	세우다, 치다	You are setting the tent.	너는 그 텐트를 치고 있다.
hard	심하게	It is raining hard now.	지금 비가 심하게 오고 있다.
noise	잡음	I am making a noise.	나는 잡음을 만들고 있다.
boil	끓이다, 삶다	My mother is boiling water.	나의 어머니는 물을 끓이고 있다.
skate	스케이트를 타다	We are skating on the ice.	우리는 얼음 위에서 스케이트를 타고 있다.
highway	고속도로	The bus goes fast on the highway.	그 버스는 고속도로에서 빨리 달린다.
future	미래	He is thinking about his future.	그는 그의 미래에 대해 생각하고 있다.
grass	풀	They are having lunch on the grass.	그들은 풀밭 위에서 점심을 먹고 있다.
tear	눈물을 흘리다	I am tearing now.	나는 지금 눈물을 흘리고 있다.
taxi	택시	Is he driving a taxi now?	그는 지금 택시를 운전하고 있니?
taste	맛이 나다	The food tastes sweet.	그 음식은 단맛이 난다.

다음 우리말 뜻에 맞는 영어 단어를 쓰시오.

1   끝마치다   _____

2   늦게까지 자지 않다   _____

3   운반하다   _____

4   열심히   _____

5   높이   _____

6   거리   _____

7   크게, 시끄럽게   _____

8   노트북   _____

9   왼쪽   _____

10   통과하다   _____

11   시험   _____

12   입다, 쓰다   _____

13   기다리다   _____

14   돌다   _____

15   많이   _____

다음 우리말 뜻에 맞는 영어 단어를 쓰시오.

1 변호사 _____

2 ~을 끄다 _____

3 넘어지다 _____

4 존경하다 _____

5 건물 _____

6 증명하다 _____

7 농구 _____

8 미끄러지다 _____

9 배우 _____

10 여행 _____

11 일하다, 작동하다 _____

12 재킷 _____

13 놓치다 _____

14 우체국 _____

15 ~을 찾다 _____

다음 우리말 뜻에 맞는 영어 단어를 쓰시오.

1	택시	_____
2	신발	_____
3	문, 출입문	_____
4	일찍	_____
5	양파	_____
6	정각에	_____
7	속하다	_____
8	돈을 내다, 지불하다	_____
9	도망가다	_____
10	받다	_____
11	짐	_____
12	무거운	_____
13	곤충	_____
14	수업, 레슨	_____
15	혼자	_____

다음 우리말 뜻에 맞는 영어 단어를 쓰시오.

1 손님　　　　　　　_____

2 수다 떨다　　　　　_____

3 짓다, 세우다　　　　_____

4 놓치다　　　　　　_____

5 운동하다　　　　　_____

6 씹다　　　　　　　_____

7 주소　　　　　　　_____

8 사실, 진실　　　　　_____

9 소음　　　　　　　_____

10 짖다　　　　　　　_____

11 식료품　　　　　　_____

12 장미　　　　　　　_____

13 기억하다　　　　　_____

14 인터넷　　　　　　_____

15 시간표　　　　　　_____

다음 우리말 뜻에 맞는 영어 단어를 쓰시오.

1 ～ 사이에 _____

2 프린터기 _____

3 점원 _____

4 오븐 _____

5 섬 _____

6 냉장고 _____

7 램프, 전등 _____

8 정원 _____

9 접시 _____

10 수프 _____

11 지폐 _____

12 주머니 _____

13 베개 _____

14 옆에 _____

15 동전 _____

다음 우리말 뜻에 맞는 영어 단어를 쓰시오.

I 시골, 나라 _____

2 한 묶음, 한 다발 _____

3 바구니 _____

4 구멍 _____

5 대학 _____

6 튤립 _____

7 조각 _____

8 애완동물 가게 _____

9 달 _____

10 과일 _____

II 새끼 고양이 _____

12 지갑 _____

13 ~ 을 통해서 _____

14 장 _____

15 창고 _____

다음 우리말 뜻에 맞는 영어 단어를 쓰시오.

1	게으른	_____
2	멋진, 시원한	_____
3	부지런한	_____
4	바깥쪽	_____
5	그림	_____
6	가져오다	_____
7	영리한	_____
8	떨어지다	_____
9	강아지	_____
10	마시다	_____
11	코트	_____
12	유용한	_____
13	유명한	_____
14	높은	_____
15	잘생긴	_____

Unit 4 Quiz

2회

다음 우리말 뜻에 맞는 영어 단어를 쓰시오.

1 배구 _____

2 더러운 _____

3 신발 _____

4 소파 _____

5 배우 _____

6 사전 _____

7 어두운 _____

8 반지 _____

9 가구 _____

10 길 _____

11 좁은 _____

12 넓은 _____

13 깊은 _____

14 밝은, 가벼운 _____

15 운동화 _____

다음 우리말 뜻에 맞는 영어 단어를 쓰시오.

1 제시간에 _____

2 소리 _____

3 해변 _____

4 만화책 _____

5 사과파이 _____

6 정보 _____

7 포크 _____

8 클래식 음악 _____

9 돈 _____

10 휴일 _____

11 쉬는 시간 _____

12 ~ 동안 _____

13 수다를 떨다 _____

14 집중하다 _____

15 질문 _____

Unit 5 Quiz 2회

다음 우리말 뜻에 맞는 영어 단어를 쓰시오.

1 소풍　_____

2 통과하다　_____

3 급우　_____

4 미래, 장래　_____

5 재미있는, 흥미로운　_____

6 진정한　_____

7 모이다　_____

8 딸기　_____

9 외식하다　_____

10 조용한　_____

11 사람　_____

12 신선한　_____

13 가지고 오다　_____

14 자르다　_____

15 건강　_____

다음 우리말 뜻에 맞는 영어 단어를 쓰시오.

1	세탁기	_____
2	숲	_____
3	액세서리	_____
4	걸치다, 입다	_____
5	벌집	_____
6	소비하다	_____
7	빵	_____
8	사막	_____
9	작가	_____
10	간식	_____
11	식사	_____
12	공간	_____
13	통증	_____
14	옷, 의류	_____
15	여행하다	_____

다음 우리말 뜻에 맞는 영어 단어를 쓰시오.

1 다른 　_____

2 샴푸 　_____

3 산소 　_____

4 종이컵 　_____

5 아픈 　_____

6 도움 　_____

7 아이디어, 생각 　_____

8 언어 　_____

9 굽다 　_____

10 색깔 　_____

11 가스 　_____

12 실수 　_____

13 서두르다 　_____

14 운, 행운 　_____

15 마당 　_____

다음 우리말 뜻에 맞는 영어 단어를 쓰시오.

1 완벽한　　　　　_____

2 대답하다　　　　_____

3 준비된　　　　　_____

4 기름진　　　　　_____

5 배구　　　　　　_____

6 던지다　　　　　_____

7 홍수　　　　　　_____

8 거의 ～ 하지 않다　_____

9 점원　　　　　　_____

10 짖다　　　　　　_____

11 터널　　　　　　_____

12 ～을 통해서　　　_____

13 시끄러운　　　　_____

14 빗질하다　　　　_____

15 운동선수　　　　_____

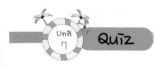
다음 우리말 뜻에 맞는 영어 단어를 쓰시오.

1 호수 _____

2 배낭 _____

3 건너다 _____

4 행동하다 _____

5 돌고래 _____

6 어려운 _____

7 머리 모양 _____

8 기자 _____

9 친절 _____

10 신용카드 _____

11 거북 _____

12 디자이너 _____

13 반바지 _____

14 코치 _____

15 언 _____

다음 우리말 뜻에 맞는 영어 단어를 쓰시오.

1 두 번 _____

2 과거 _____

3 휴대폰 _____

4 부츠 _____

5 거짓말하다 _____

6 고치다 _____

7 마음 _____

8 주변 _____

9 죽다 _____

10 연설 _____

11 빗질하다 _____

12 누군가 _____

13 노크하다 _____

14 오르다 _____

15 껴안다 _____

다음 우리말 뜻에 맞는 영어 단어를 쓰시오.

1   수다를 떨다 _____

2   ~에 속하다 _____

3   기계 _____

4   ~을 찾다 _____

5   서로 _____

6   뜨개질하다 _____

7   치다, 세우다 _____

8   먹이를 주다 _____

9   외국인 _____

10 줄넘기하다 _____

11 고속도로 _____

12 심하게 _____

13 잡음 _____

14 삶다, 끓이다 _____

15 거짓말하다, 눕다 _____

Answer Key

| Unit 1 | Quiz 1회 | p. 10 |

1 finish 2 stay up late 3 carry 4 hard
5 high 6 street 7 loudly 8 laptop 9 left
10 pass 11. exam 12 wear 13 wait for
14 turn to 15 a lot

| Unit 1 | Quiz 2회 | p. 11 |

1 lawyer 2 turn off 3 fall down
4 respect 5 building 6 prove
7 basketball 8 slip 9 actor 10 trip
11 work 12 jacket 13 miss
14 post office 15 look for

| Unit 2 | Quiz 1회 | p. 12 |

1 taxi 2 shoes 3 gate 4 early 5 onion
6 on time 7 belong 8 pay 9 run away
10 receive 11 luggage 12 heavy
13 insect 14 lesson 15 alone

| Unit 2 | Quiz 2회 | p. 13 |

1 guest 2 chat 3 build 4 miss
5 exercise 6 chew 7 address 8 truth
9 noise 10 bark 11 grocery 12 rose
13 remember 14 Internet 15 time table

| Unit 3 | Quiz 1회 | p. 14 |

1 between 2 printer 3 clerk 4 oven
5 island 6 refrigerator 7 lamp 8 garden
9 plate 10 soup 11 bill 12 pocket
13 pillow 14 beside 15 coin

| Unit 3 | Quiz 2회 | p. 15 |

1 country 2 a bunch of 3 basket
4 hole 5 university 6 tulip 7 piece
8 pet shop 9 moon 10 fruit 11 kitten
12 purse 13 through 14 sheet
15 storage

| Unit 4 | Quiz 1회 | p. 16 |

1 lazy 2 cool 3 diligent 4 outside
5 painting 6 bring 7 smart 8 fall
9 puppy 10 drink 11 coat 12 useful
13 famous 14 high 15 handsome

| Unit 4 | Quiz 2회 | p. 17 |

1 volleyball 2 dirty 3 shoes 4 sofa
5 actor 6 dictionary 7 dark 8 ring
9 furniture 10 road 11narrow 12 wide
13 deep 14 light 15 sneakers

Unit 5 ı Quiz 1회   p. 18

1 on time   2 sound   3 beach
4 comic book   5 apple pie   6 information
7 fork   8 classical music   9 money
10 holiday   11 break   12 during   13 chat
14 attention   15 question

Unit 5 ı Quiz 2회   p. 19

1 picnic   2 pass   3 classmate   4 future
5 interesting   6 true   7 get together
8 strawberry   9 eat out   10 quiet
11 person   12 fresh   13 bring   14 cut
15 health

Unit 6 ı Quiz 1회   p. 20

1 washing machine   2 forest
3 accessory   4 wear   5 hive   6 spend
7 bread   8 desert   9 writer   10 snack
11 meal   12 space   13 pain   14 cloth
15 travel

Unit 6 ı Quiz 2회   p. 21

1 different   2 shampoo   3 oxygen
4 paper cup   5 sick   6 help   7 idea
8 language   9 bake   10 color   11 gas
12 mistake   13 hurry   14 luck   15 yard

Unit 7 ı Quiz 1회   p. 22

1 perfect   2 answer   3 ready   4 fatty

5 volleyball   6 pitch   7 flood   8 hardly
9 clerk   10 bark   11 tunnel   12 through
13 loud   14 comb   15 athlete

Unit 7 ı Quiz 2회   p. 23

1 lake   2 backpack   3 cross   4 act
5 dolphin   6 difficult   7 hair style
8 reporter   9 kindness   10 credit card
11 turtle   12 designer   13 shorts
14 coach   15 frozen

Unit 8 ı Quiz 1회   p. 24

1 twice   2 past   3 cell phone   4 boots
5 lie   6 fix   7 mind   8 around   9 die
10 speech   11 brush   12 someone
13 knock   14 climb   15 hug

Unit 8 ı Quiz 2회   p. 25

1 chat   2 belong   3 machine   4 look for
5 each other   6 knit   7 set   8 feed
9 foreigner   10 jump rope   11 highway
12 hard   13 noise   14 boil   15 lie

Memo

초등 영어 교재의 베스트셀러

초등 영어 문법 실력 쌓기!

Grammar Builder

You Are the Only One!

2

Introduction Grammar Builder는?

이 책의 성격

문법 개념 설명부터 마무리 확인까지 실용 문제로 구성된 기본 영어 문법서

이 책의 학습 목표 및 특징

• 다양하고 많은 문제를 통해 실전 문법을 익히고 영어 교과 과정을 대비한다.

• 이해하기 쉽게 설명한 문법의 개념과 원리를 바탕으로 문제를 통해 실력을 향상시킨다.

• 핵심 문법 개념을 이해하고 점진적으로 확장된 문제를 통해 문법 원리를 익힌다.

• 문법 학습뿐만 아니라 문장 패턴 학습과 기초 문장 영작을 통해 문장 쓰기를 훈련한다.

• 서술형 비중이 커지는 추세를 반영하여 학업 성취도 및 서술형 평가를 대비한다.

이 책에 대한 세부 사항

• 문법 개념 설명부터 마무리 확인까지 문제 형식으로 구성하여 실전에 강하도록 하였다.

• 선택형 문제, 단답형 쓰기, 문장 패턴 쓰기로 확장하며 실력을 향상하도록 구성하였다.

• 단어와 문장을 정리하여 사전에 학습함으로 자연스럽게 문법 학습이 이루어지도록 하였다.

• 실전 문제와 서술형 문제를 강화하여 문법 개념과 원리를 응용할 수 있도록 하였다.

이 책을 활용한 영어 문법 실력 쌓기

1. 문법 학습 전 정리된 단어와 문장을 먼저 예습한다.

   – 단어와 문장을 알면 어렵게 느껴지는 문법도 쉽게 학습할 수 있다.

2. 문법은 이해+암기이다. 필요한 문법 사항은 암기한다.

   – 문법의 쓰임과 역할을 이해하고 암기하여 필요할 때 적용하는 것이 좋다.

3. 문법을 학습할 때 예문을 통해 문법 개념을 학습한다.

   – 예문을 문법적으로 파악하면 문장이 복잡해도 쉽게 이해할 수 있다.

4. 문제를 푸는 것으로 끝내지 않고 대화나 글로 마무리한다.

   – 문법을 배우는 이유는 글을 이해하고 쓸 수 있는 능력을 갖추기 위한 것이다.

Grammar Series Contents

contents

About This Book 구성 및 특징

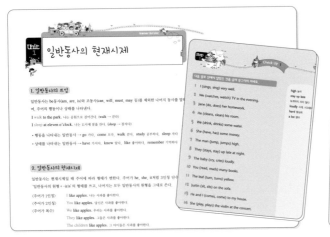

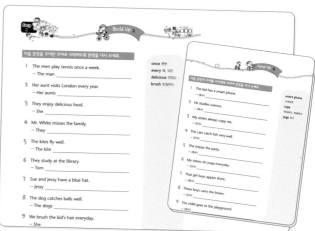

① ② ③ ④

1. Unit별 핵심 문법 개념 정리

Unit별 학습목표를 제시하여 중점 사항을 파악하도록 하였고, 기초적인 문법 사항을 쉽게 이해할 수 있도록 설명하여 문법 개념 이해를 돕습니다. 또한 다양한 예문을 통해 문법 원리 학습을 적용하여 이해하도록 하였습니다.

2. Step 1 – Check Up

학습목표와 핵심문법 개념에 대한 기초적인 확인 문제로 구성하여 문법 원리를 문제를 통해서 익히도록 구성하였습니다. 스스로 풀어보면서 반복 학습을 통해 문법의 규칙을 이해하도록 하였습니다.

3. Step 2 – Build Up

다양한 형식의 다소 난이도 있는 문제로 구성하여 앞에서 배운 내용을 복습하며 문법 원리를 익히도록 하였습니다. 학습한 내용을 본격적으로 적용하고 응용해 보면서 다양한 유형을 연습하도록 하였습니다.

4. Step 3 – Jump Up

핵심 문법 개념을 스스로 정리해 보도록 하여 이해도를 확인하고 보완하도록 하였으며 확장형 응용문제를 통해 학습 목표를 성취하도록 하였습니다. 또한 영작문 실력이 향상되도록 서술형 문제 위주로 구성하였습니다.

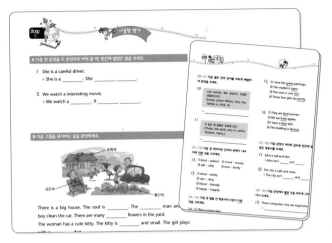
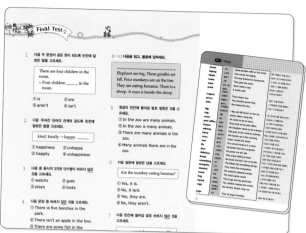

5. Step 4 – 실전 평가

Unit별 핵심 문법 개념과 다양한 문제로 익힌 문법 사항을 마무리 테스트로 구성하여 스스로 점검해 보도록 하였습니다. 이를 통해 문법 문제에 대한 응용력을 키우고 시험 유형에 대비하도록 하였습니다.

6. Step 5 – 서술평 평가

점점 서술형 비중이 커지는 추세를 반영하여 영작문 위주로 구성된 Unit별 종합 문제를 풀어보면서 Unit을 정리하고 학업성취도 평가 및 서술형 평가를 대비하도록 하였습니다.

7. Final Test

본 교재를 통해서 배운 핵심 문법 개념과 문법 사항을 종합평가로 풀어보면서 정리하고 마무리하도록 하였습니다. 종합적으로 배운 내용을 확인하고 점검하도록 하였습니다.

8. Words in Grammar

본 교재의 본문에 사용된 단어들과 문장을 정리하여 문법 학습에 활용하도록 하였습니다. 예습으로 단어를 학습하고 학습 집중도를 올리도록 활용하는 것이 좋습니다.

Curriculum

Book	Month	Week	Hour	Unit	
1	1	1	1	1. 문장의 기본 구성	Words 활용
			2		서술형 평가
		2	1	2. 셀 수 있는 명사	Words 활용
			2		서술형 평가
		3	1	3. 셀 수 없는 명사	Words 활용
			2		서술형 평가
		4	1	4. 관사	Words 활용
			2		서술형 평가
	2	1	1	5. 인칭대명사와 격변화	Words 활용
			2		서술형 평가
		2	1	6. 지시대명사, 지시형용사	Words 활용
			2		서술형 평가
		3	1	7. be동사의 현재시제	Words 활용
			2		서술형 평가
		4	1	8. be동사의 부정문, 의문문	Words 활용
			2		서술형 평가
2	3	1	1	1. 일반동사의 현재시제	Words 활용
			2		서술형 평가
		2	1	2. 일반동사의 부정문, 의문문	Words 활용
			2		서술형 평가
		3	1	3. There is/are, 비인칭주어 it	Words 활용
			2		서술형 평가
		4	1	4. 형용사	Words 활용
			2		서술형 평가
	4	1	1	5. Some, Any, All, Every	Words 활용
			2		서술형 평가
		2	1	6. 수량형용사	Words 활용
			2		서술형 평가
		3	1	7. 부사	Words 활용
			2		서술형 평가
		4	1	8. 현재진행형	Words 활용
			2		서술형 평가
3	5	1	1	1. 기수와 서수	Words 활용
			2		서술형 평가
		2	1	2. 부정대명사, 재귀대명사	Words 활용
			2		서술형 평가
		3	1	3. 비교 구문	Words 활용
			2		서술형 평가
		4	1	4. 조동사	Words 활용
			2		서술형 평가

Grammar Builder 시리즈는 총 5권으로 구성되어 있으며, 권당 8주(2개월) 16차시(Unit당 2차시 수업)로 학습할 수 있도록 구성하였습니다. 주 2회 수업을 기준으로 하였으며 학습자와 학습 시간에 따라 변경이 가능합니다.

Book	Month	Week	Hour	Unit	
3	6	1	1	5. 동사의 과거시제	Words 활용
			2		서술형 평가
		2	1	6. 과거시제의 부정문, 의문문	Words 활용
			2		서술형 평가
		3	1	7. 과거진행형	Words 활용
			2		서술형 평가
		4	1	8. 동사의 미래시제	Words 활용
			2		서술형 평가
4	7	1	1	1. 의문사 의문문	Words 활용
			2		서술형 평가
		2	1	2. 의문대명사와 의문형용사	Words 활용
			2		서술형 평가
		3	1	3. 의문부사	Words 활용
			2		서술형 평가
		4	1	4. 명령문	Words 활용
			2		서술형 평가
	8	1	1	5. 감탄문	Words 활용
			2		서술형 평가
		2	1	6. 접속사	Words 활용
			2		서술형 평가
		3	1	7. 전치사	Words 활용
			2		서술형 평가
		4	1	8. 부정의문문, 부가의문문	Words 활용
			2		서술형 평가
5	9	1	1	1. to부정사	Words 활용
			2		서술형 평가
		2	1	2. 동명사	Words 활용
			2		서술형 평가
		3	1	3. 현재분사와 과거분사	Words 활용
			2		서술형 평가
		4	1	4. 문장의 형식 1	Words 활용
			2		서술형 평가
	10	1	1	5. 문장의 형식 2	Words 활용
			2		서술형 평가
		2	1	6. 현재완료	Words 활용
			2		서술형 평가
		3	1	7. 수동태	Words 활용
			2		서술형 평가
		4	1	8. 관계대명사	Words 활용
			2		서술형 평가

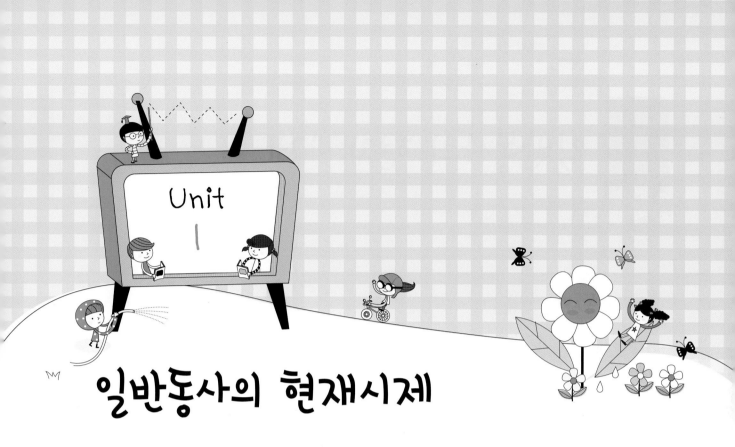

일반동사의 현재시제

일반동사 현재시제의 의미와 쓰임을 이해할 수 있다.

일반동사의 3인칭 단수 현재형을 활용할 수 있다.

일반동사란 주어의 행동이나 상태를 나타내는 말로, 행동을 나타내는 일반동사에는 go(가다), eat(먹다), walk(걷다) 등이 있으며 상태를 나타내는 일반동사에는 have (가지다), know(알다), like(좋아하다) 등이 있어요. 일반 동사가 쓰인 문장이 현재 시제일 때 일반동사는 주어에 따라 그 형태가 변해요.

Unit 1 · 일반동사의 현재시제

1. 일반동사의 쓰임

일반동사는 be동사(am, are, is)와 조동사(can, will, must, may 등)를 제외한 나머지 동사를 말하며, 주어의 행동이나 상태를 나타낸다.

I walk to the park. 나는 공원으로 걸어간다. (walk → 걷다)

I sleep at eleven o'clock. 나는 11시에 잠을 잔다. (sleep → 잠자다)

• 행동을 나타내는 일반동사 → go 가다, come 오다, walk 걷다, study 공부하다, sleep 자다

• 상태를 나타내는 일반동사 → have 가지다, know 알다, like 좋아하다, remember 기억하다

2. 일반동사의 현재시제

일반동사는 현재시제일 때 주어에 따라 형태가 변한다. 주어가 he, she, it처럼 3인칭 단수일 때 '일반동사의 원형＋-(e)s'의 형태를 쓰고, 나머지는 모두 일반동사의 원형을 그대로 쓴다.

〈주어가 1인칭〉 I like apples. 나는 사과를 좋아한다.

〈주어가 2인칭〉 You like apples. 당신은 사과를 좋아한다.

〈주어가 복수〉 We like apples. 우리는 사과를 좋아한다.

They like apples. 그들은 사과를 좋아한다.

The children like apples. 그 아이들은 사과를 좋아한다.

〈주어가 3인칭 단수〉 He likes apples. 그는 사과를 좋아한다.

She likes apples. 그녀는 사과를 좋아한다.

John likes apples. John은 사과를 좋아한다.

일반 동사의 원형이란?
'walks, walking, walked' 등은 모두 walk (걷다)가
변형된 것이다. 이렇게 walk처럼 일반 동사의 원래의 형태를
동사원형이라고 한다.

Pop Quiz

Ⅰ. 다음 문장에서 일반동사를 찾아 동그라미 하세요.

❶ We read books after school. ❷ He drinks milk every morning.

3. 일반동사의 3인칭 단수형

문장의 주어가 3인칭 단수이고, 시제가 현재일 때 일반동사에 -s, -es를 붙여 3인칭 단수형으로 나타낸다.

(1) 규칙 변화: 대부분의 동사는 규칙적으로 변한다.

만드는 법		예
대부분의 동사	+s를 붙인다.	come 오다 → comes start 시작하다 → starts choose 선택하다 → chooses
-s, -sh, -ch, -x, -o로 끝나는 동사	+es를 붙인다.	mix 섞다 → mixes go 가다 → goes do 하다 → does kiss 키스하다 → kisses wash 씻다 → washes teach 가르치다 → teaches
자음+y로 끝나는 동사	-y를 i로 바꾸고 +es를 붙인다.	study 공부하다 → studies carry 운반하다 → carries
모음+y로 끝나는 동사	+s를 붙인다.	pay 지불하다 → pays say 말하다 → says

(2) 불규칙 변화: 규칙이 적용되지 않는 동사　have → has

My sister gets up at six o'clock. 나의 언니는 6시에 일어난다.

She goes to school by bus. 그녀는 버스로 학교에 간다.

She does her homework. 그녀는 그녀의 숙제를 한다.

He has lunch at twelve. 그는 12시에 점심을 먹는다.

4. 일반동사의 여러 가지 의미

여러 가지 뜻을 가지는 일반동사가 있는데, 정확한 뜻은 문장 속에서 파악해야 한다.

have	look	get	make
❶ 가지다	❶ 보다	❶ 얻다	❶ 만들다
❷ 먹다	❷ 조사하다	❷ 도착하다	❷ 생산하다
❸ 경험하다	❸ ~처럼 보이다	❸ ~이 되어지다	❸ ~을 하게 하다

I have dinner.(= I eat dinner.) 나는 저녁을 먹는다. (먹다)

I have a big ball. 나는 큰 공을 가지고 있다. (가지다)

He looks at the bear. 나는 그 곰을 본다. (보다)

He looks happy. 그는 행복해 보인다. (~처럼 보인다)

Pop Quiz　　2. 다음 괄호 안에서 알맞은 것을 고르세요.

❶ He (like, likes) dogs.　　❷ We (go, goes) to school.

다음 괄호 안에서 알맞은 것을 골라 동그라미 하세요.

1 I (sings, sing) very well.

2 We (watches, watch) TV in the evening.

3 Jane (do, does) her homework.

4 He (cleans, clean) his room.

5 We (drink, drinks) some water.

6 She (have, has) some money.

7 The man (jump, jumps) high.

8 They (stays, stay) up late at night.

9 The baby (cry, cries) loudly.

10 You (read, reads) many books.

11 The leaf (turn, turns) yellow.

12 Justin (sit, sits) on the sofa.

13 He and she (comes, come) to my house.

14 She (play, plays) the violin at the concert.

15 My father (works, work) very hard.

16 It (snows, snow) a lot in winter.

high 높이

stay up late
늦게까지 자지 않다

loudly 크게, 시끄럽게

hard 열심히

a lot 많이

다음 괄호 안에서 알맞은 것을 골라 동그라미 하세요.

street 거리
carry 운반하다
laptop 노트북
finish 끝마치다
pass 통과하다
exam 시험

1 He (helps, help) the old man.

2 Many people (walks, walk) on the street.

3 Brian (gets, get) on the bus.

4 My mom and I (have, has) dinner at six o'clock.

5 The woman (eat, eats) a sandwich.

6 My parents (know, knows) my friends.

7 Dan (carry, carries) his laptop.

8 The child (go, goes) to bed at ten.

9 He and you (enjoy, enjoys) the party.

10 He (buy, buys) some flowers for his wife.

11 The boys (finish, finishes) their homework.

12 My sister (stay, stays) in New York.

13 John (see, sees) a dog in the park.

14 They (passes, pass) the exam.

15 He (makes, make) some cookies.

16 Those children (studies, study) math.

Check Up 3

다음 괄호 안에서 알맞은 말을 골라 동그라미 하세요.

1 (My dad, You, We) makes a toy house.

2 (Paul, He, They) come home early.

3 (We, You, She) lives in Seoul.

4 (I, They, Tom) wears a cap.

5 (You, I, Jim) sees many people in the park.

6 (You, Dan and Jane, Paul) waits for us.

7 (He, We, He and she) turns to the left.

8 (He, They, She) look sleepy.

9 (Mary, Jim and Alex, It) watch the movie.

10 (He, She, We) look for a key.

11 (My uncle, My aunts, They) forgets it.

12 (She, We, He and she) turns off the TV.

13 (We, It, They) works well.

14 (Her friend, You, He) close the window.

15 (She, He, He and she) swim in the pool.

16 (Judy and Sam, Ann, I) walks to the market.

wear 입다, 쓰다
wait for 기다리다
turn 돌다
left 왼쪽
look for ~을 찾다
turn off ~을 끄다
work 일하다, 작동하다

다음 괄호 안에서 알맞은 말을 골라 동그라미 하세요.

building 건물
prove 증명하다
miss 놓치다
fall down 넘어지다
trip 여행

1 (She, They, The man) go to the station.

2 (His friends, His friend) says hello to her.

3 (Mike and John, Minho, She) enter the building.

4 (My dad, He and she) solves the problem.

5 (The scientists, The scientist) prove that.

6 (They, The girl, He) understand a question.

7 (Minho, His sister, We) win the game.

8 (He, They, You) gets up late in the morning.

9 (The woman, The women) shows the photo to me.

10 (She, You, They) plays the piano.

11 (A year, Years) has twelve months.

12 (She, The children) misses the bus.

13 (He, The babies) cry all day long.

14 (You and I, He, She) look at the map.

15 (Amy, Tony, I) fall down on the ice.

16 (They, I, Jessica) takes a long trip.

다음 주어진 동사를 이용해 문장을 완성하세요.

1 My friend _____ good movies. (watch)

2 The airplane _____ high. (fly)

3 He _____ a song. (sing)

4 She _____ a big house. (have)

5 They _____ on the bench. (sit)

6 Janet and Tom _____ at the sky. (look)

7 She _____ a jacket. (wear)

8 They _____ us to their house. (invite)

9 Peter _____ a taxi. (drive)

10 My grandfather _____ in the room. (sleep)

11 Those horses _____ very fast. (run)

12 Some children _____ basketball. (play)

13 He _____ a model airplane. (make)

14 The student _____ for a school bus. (wait)

15 My son _____ home after school. (come)

16 My parents _____ all my friends. (know)

jacket 재킷
basketball 농구

다음 주어진 동사를 이용해 문장을 완성하세요.

1 My teacher ＿＿＿＿＿ some books. (carry)

2 They ＿＿＿＿＿ at the post office. (work)

3 It ＿＿＿＿＿ a lot in summer. (rain)

4 His daughter ＿＿＿＿＿ a lawyer. (meet)

5 The boy ＿＿＿＿＿ the old man. (help)

6 A lot of people ＿＿＿＿＿ on the street. (walk)

7 Mrs. White ＿＿＿＿＿ two cats. (have)

8 She ＿＿＿＿＿ her English teacher. (like)

9 The girl ＿＿＿＿＿ her homework. (do)

10 Suji ＿＿＿＿＿ to her work by subway. (go)

11 My parents often ＿＿＿＿＿ coffee. (drink)

12 That man ＿＿＿＿＿ a letter to his wife. (write)

13 The baby ＿＿＿＿＿ on the bed. (sleep)

14 He ＿＿＿＿＿ up in the morning. (hurry)

15 Sora ＿＿＿＿＿ TV after dinner. (watch)

16 Those girls always ＿＿＿＿＿ clothes together. (buy)

post office 우체국
lawyer 변호사
subway 지하철
often 자주, 종종
hurry 서두르다
always 항상
clothes 옷

다음 문장에서 일반동사를 찾아 바르게 고쳐 쓰세요.

cross 건너다
jeans 청바지
end 끝나다
fix 고치다
pass 건네주다

1 His mother make some cookies. → _____

2 Sumi play the piano well. → _____

3 They closes their eyes. → _____

4 He wash his hair every morning. → _____

5 Tom and Jessica crosses the street. → _____

6 They enjoys the party. → _____

7 My mother buy the jeans for me. → _____

8 The concert end at three o'clock. → _____

9 The movie begin at 7:30. → _____

10 They carries the chairs. → _____

11 My brother clean the room. → _____

12 Tom haves breakfast at eight. → _____

13 My teacher pay the money. → _____

14 My father fixs the computer. → _____

15 Tom and his brother reads books. → _____

16 He pass me the salt. → _____

다음 문장을 주어진 주어로 시작하도록 문장을 다시 쓰세요.

1 The men play tennis once a week.

→ The man _____

2 Her aunt visits London every year.

→ Her aunts _____

3 They enjoy delicious food.

→ She _____

4 Mr. White misses the family.

→ They _____

5 The kites fly well.

→ The kite _____

6 They study in the library.

→ Tom _____

7 Sue and Jessy have a blue hat.

→ Jessy _____

8 The dog catches balls well.

→ The dogs _____

9 We brush the kid's hair everyday.

→ She _____

10 My mother cooks in the morning.

→ My sisters _____

once 한번
every 매, 모든
delicious 맛있는
brush 빗질하다

다음 괄호 안에 주어진 주어로 바꾸어 문장을 다시 쓰세요.

1 The boy knows them. (The boys)

→ _____

2 The child runs to the park. (The children)

→ _____

3 The girls wear glasses. (The girl)

→ _____

4 He has two daughters. (They)

→ _____

5 The babies eat something all day. (The baby)

→ _____

6 The hunters look for deer. (The hunter)

→ _____

7 The sun shines in the sky. (The stars)

→ _____

8 They watch TV after lunch. (Suji)

→ _____

9 My mom sells clothes at the market. (My parents)

→ _____

10 They catch five mosquitoes. (He)

→ _____

다음 빈칸에 알맞은 말을 쓰세요.

1 일반동사란, 주어의 _____이나 _____를 나타내는 동사이다.

• _____을 나타내는 동사: **go** 가다, **come** 오다, **walk** 걷다, **study** 공부하다, **sleep** 자다

• _____를 나타내는 동사: **have** 가지다, **know** 알다, **like** 좋아하다, **remember** 기억하다

2 일반동사의 현재시제

일반동사는 현재시제일 때 주어에 따라 형태가 변한다. 주어가 **he, she, it**처럼 _____일 때 '일반동사의 원형 + -(e)s'의 형태를 쓰고, 나머지는 모두 일반동사의 _____을 쓴다.

3 일반동사의 3인칭 단수형

(1) **규칙 변화**: 일반동사에 _____나 _____를 붙여 만든다.

만드는 법		예
대부분의 동사	+s를 붙인다.	come → _____
-s, -sh, -ch, -x, -o로 끝나는 동사	+es를 붙인다.	kiss → kiss**es** wash → _____ teach → teach**es** mix → mix**es** do → _____
자음+y로 끝나는 동사	-y를 ____로 바꾸고 +es를 붙인다.	study → studi**es**
모음+y로 끝나는 동사	+s를 붙인다.	say → _____

(2) **불규칙 변화**: 규칙이 적용되지 않는 동사로, **have**의 3인칭 단수형은 _____이다.

다음 문장에서 밑줄 친 부분을 바르게 고쳐 쓰세요.

miss 그리워하다
classical 고전의
twice 두 번
wood 목재

1 Grandpa <u>gos</u> to the mountain. → _____

2 Sue <u>studys</u> in Korea. → _____

3 He <u>plais</u> baseball on Saturdays. → _____

4 She <u>buy</u> fruits at the store. → _____

5 Scott <u>miss</u> his friends. → _____

6 Jim <u>have</u> three brothers. → _____

7 The child <u>cry</u> in the room. → _____

8 John <u>watch</u> classical movies. → _____

9 An eagle <u>flys</u> in the sky. → _____

10 She <u>wash</u> her face twice a day. → _____

11 The concert <u>finish</u> at five p.m. → _____

12 Ms. Johnes <u>teach</u> English at school. → _____

13 The truck <u>carrys</u> wood. → _____

14 Her brother <u>fixs</u> his bike. → _____

15 He <u>dos</u> his homework. → _____

16 The baby <u>kiss</u> the doll. → _____

다음 문장에서 동사 부분을 바르게 고쳐 문장을 다시 쓰세요.

1 She haves a beautiful dress.

→ _____

2 The kid play with his friends.

→ _____

3 The birds sits in the tree.

→ _____

4 Mr. Brown work at a bank.

→ _____

5 They swims in the river.

→ _____

6 The boys plays basketball after school.

→ _____

7 He and she drinks milk every morning.

→ _____

8 John and I meets her at the bus stop.

→ _____

9 My sister write a postcard.

→ _____

10 The children rides bikes in the park.

→ _____

after school
방과 후에

bus stop 버스정류장

다음 문장의 주어를 지시대로 바꾸어 문장을 다시 쓰세요.

1 The kid has a smart phone.

   → (복수) _____

2 He studies science.

   → (복수) _____

3 My brothers always copy me.

   → (단수) _____

4 The cats catch fish very well.

   → (단수) _____

5 She enjoys the party.

   → (복수) _____

6 My sisters do yoga everyday.

   → (단수) _____

7 That girl buys apples there.

   → (복수) _____

8 These boys carry the boxes.

   → (단수) _____

9 The child goes to the playground.

   → (복수) _____

10 The women watch a movie every weekend.

   → (단수) _____

---

smart phone

스마트폰

copy

따라하다, 복제하다

yoga 요가

일반동사의 현재시제 • **29**

[1~3] 다음 중 동사원형과 3인칭 단수 현재형이 바르게 짝지어지지 <u>않은</u> 것을 고르세요.

1
① say – says
② play – plays
③ enjoy – enjoys
④ study – studys

2
① come – comes
② have – haves
③ go – goes
④ do – does

3
① miss – misses
② fix – fixes
③ finish – finishs
④ wash – washes

[4~5] 다음 빈칸에 들어갈 말로 알맞은 것을 고르세요.

4 _____ teaches science at school.
① I
② You
③ Mrs. Lee
④ You and Judy

5 _____ sleep well every night.
① I
② He
③ She
④ The baby

[6~7] 다음 괄호 안에서 알맞은 말을 고르세요.

6 He (ride / rides) a bike.

7 Minho and Jinsu (do / does) their homework together.

[8~9] 다음 중 밑줄 친 부분이 바른 것을 고르세요.

8
① Mr. Smith <u>teach</u> English.
② The man <u>live</u> with his family.
③ She <u>speaks</u> English well.
④ His brother <u>read</u> many books.

9
① He and I <u>likes</u> baseball.
② She <u>visit</u> us on Sundays.
③ We <u>comes</u> home at three.
④ They <u>know</u> her phone number.

[10~11] 다음 밑줄 친 동사의 형태가 바른 것끼리 짝지어진 것을 고르세요.

10
· My brother <u>buy</u> a comic book.
· The children <u>hug</u> each other.

① buy - hug
② buy - hugs
③ buys - hug
④ buys - hugs

11

> · My dad <u>drive</u> his car.
> · Tom <u>walk</u> to school.

① drive – walk

② drive – walks

③ drives – walk

④ drives – walks

[12~13] 다음 괄호 안의 동사를 알맞은 형태로 바꿔 쓰세요.

12 We ＿＿＿＿＿＿ dinner at seven.
           (have)

13 She ＿＿＿＿＿＿ some cookies.
           (make)

[14~15] 다음 빈칸에 들어갈 말로 알맞지 <u>않은</u> 것을 고르세요.

14 He ＿＿＿＿＿ his bag.
    ① makes   ② likes
    ③ selles   ④ gives

15 The man ＿＿＿＿＿ the piano.
    ① plays   ② likes
    ③ loves   ④ carrys

[16~18] 다음 중 바르지 <u>않은</u> 문장을 고르세요.

16 ① The child cries in his room.
    ② These boys swim in the river.
    ③ Hana watchs classical movies.
    ④ An eagle flies in the sky.

17 ① He studies science.
    ② My sisters always copy me.
    ③ The cats catch fish very well.
    ④ She enjoy the party.

18 ① They sleeps in the room.
    ② A year has twelve months.
    ③ She misses the bus.
    ④ The babies cry all day long.

[19~20] 다음 문장을 제시된 주어로 시작하도록 바꾸어 쓰세요.

19 She looks at the pictures.
    → They ＿＿＿＿＿＿＿＿＿＿

20 They fix the computer.
    → My brother ＿＿＿＿＿＿＿＿＿

A 다음 Julie의 시간표를 보고, 빈칸에 알맞은 말을 쓰세요.

	Monday	Tuesday	Wednesday
1	English	Korean	English
2	Math	History	Korean
3	Science	Art	Math
4	Music ♥		P.E.

1 Julie _____ science on Monday. Julie는 월요일에 과학을 공부한다.

2 Julie _____ three classes on Tuesday. Julie는 화요일에 3교시 수업이다.

3 Julie _____ music very much. Julie는 음악을 아주 많이 좋아한다.

B 다음 질문에 맞게 빈칸에 알맞은 말을 쓰세요.

1 다음은 Amy의 일과이다. 빈칸에 알맞은 일반동사를 쓰세요.

I get up at 7. I _____ my face and hair in the morning. I _____ breakfast at 7:30. I walk to school. I come home at 3. I _____ my homework before dinner. I _____ dinner at 7 with my family. I _____ TV after dinner. I _____ to bed at 10.

2 위 내용을 바탕으로 Amy의 오빠의 일과를 소개하는 글을 완성하세요.

He gets up at 6. He _____ his face and hair in the morning. He _____ breakfast at 6:30. He _____ to school by bus. He comes home at 7. He _____ dinner at 7 with his family. He _____ English and math after dinner. He _____ to bed at 12.

일반동사의 부정문, 의문문

일반동사 현재시제의 긍정문을 이해하고 활용할 수 있다.

일반동사 현재시제의 의문문을 이해하고 활용할 수 있다.

일반동사 현재시제의 의문문에 대답하는 방법을 이해할 수 있다.

'~하지 않다'라는 부정의 말이 들어간 문장을 부정문이라고 해요. 일반동사의 부정문은 일반동사 바로 앞에 don't를 붙이는데, 주어가 3인칭 단수이면 doesn't를 붙여 만들고 일반동사는 동사원형을 써요.

'~하니?'라고 물어보는 문장을 의문문이라고 하며, 주어 앞에 Do나 Does를 붙이고 문장 맨 끝에 물음표를 붙여요. 뒤에 나오는 일반동사는 동사원형을 써요.

Unit 2

일반동사의 부정문, 의문문

1. 일반동사의 부정문 (1)

'~하지 않다'라고 부정의 말이 들어간 문장을 부정문이라고 한다. 주어가 1, 2인칭 단수 또는 복수, 3인칭 복수인 경우에 일반동사 바로 앞에 don't(= do not)를 붙여 부정문을 만든다.

I like grapes. 나는 포도를 좋아한다.

→ I don't(= do not) like grapes. 나는 포도를 좋아하지 않는다.

They have lunch. 그들은 점심을 먹는다.

→ They don't(= do not) have lunch. 그들은 점심을 먹지 않는다.

2. 일반동사의 부정문 (2)

'주어가 3인칭 단수이면 doesn't(= does not)를 붙여 만든다. 뒤에 오는 일반동사는 -s나 -es가 붙지 않은 동사원형을 쓴다.

He likes baseball. 그는 야구를 좋아한다.

→ He doesn't(= does not) like baseball. (○) 그는 야구를 좋아하지 않는다.

　He doesn't(= does not) likes baseball. (×)

	주어(단수)	do(es)+not	축약형	주어(복수)	do(es)+not	축약형
1인칭	I	do not	don't	We	do not	don't
2인칭	You			You		
3인칭	He She It	does not	doesn't	They		

▶ **참고**_ 우리말에서는 '…도 ~하다.'라고 할 때 긍정문이나 부정문에 동일한 말이 사용되지만 영어에서는 긍정문에서는 too, 부정문에서는 either로 구분해서 쓴다.

too(긍정문에 사용)	either(부정문에 사용)
A: I like summer. 나는 여름을 좋아해.	*A:* I don't like summer. 나는 여름을 좋아하지 않아.
B: I like summer, too. 나도 역시 여름을 좋아해.	*B:* I don't like summer, either. 나도 역시 여름을 좋아하지 않아.

Pop Quiz Ⅰ. 다음 괄호 안에서 알맞은 것을 고르세요.
❶ I (don't, doesn't) like him.   ❷ He (don't, doesn't) have dinner.

3. 일반동사의 의문문 (1)

'~하니?'라고 물어보는 문장이 의문문이다. 주어가 1, 2인칭 단수 또는 복수, 3인칭 복수인 경우에 주어 앞에 Do를 붙이고 문장 맨 끝에 물음표(?)를 붙여 의문문을 만든다.

　　　You like juice. 너는 주스를 좋아한다.

[의문문]　Do you like juice? 너는 주스를 좋아하니?

4. 일반동사의 의문문 (2)

주어가 3인칭 단수인 경우에 주어 앞에 Does를 붙이고 문장 맨 끝에 물음표(?)를 붙여 의문문을 만든다. 뒤에 오는 일반동사는 -s나 -es가 붙지 않은 동사원형을 쓴다.

　　　He lives in Seoul. 그는 서울에 산다.

[의문문]　Does he live in Seoul? (○) 그는 서울에 사니?

　　　Does he lives in Seoul? (×)

5. 일반동사 의문문의 대답

대답이 긍정이면 Yes, 부정이면 No를 이용하여 주어와 do 또는 does를 사용하여 답한다. 또한 부정의 대답은 축약형을 사용한다.

의문문	긍정의 대답	부정의 대답
Do you like milk?	Yes, I do.	No, I don't.
Does he live in Seoul?	Yes, he does.	No, he doesn't.

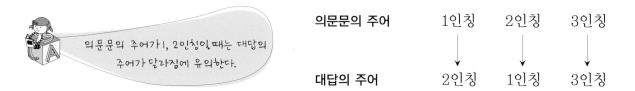

의문문의 주어가 1, 2인칭일 때는 대답의 주어가 달라짐에 유의한다.

의문문의 주어	1인칭	2인칭	3인칭
	↓	↓	↓
대답의 주어	2인칭	1인칭	3인칭

• 의문문에 대해 대답할 때, 주어는 항상 대명사로 받는다. 주어가 단수명사인 경우 he, she, it으로, 복수명사인 경우 they로 받는다.

Does Brian like computer games? – Yes, he does. / No, he doesn't.
Brian은 컴퓨터 게임을 좋아하니?   응, 그래.   아니, 그렇지 않아.

Do John and Tom play soccer? – Yes, they do. / No, they don't.
John과 Tom은 축구를 하니?   응, 그래.   아니, 그렇지 않아.

> **Pop Quiz** 2. 다음 괄호 안에서 알맞은 것을 고르세요.
> ❶ (Do, Does) you walk there?   ❷ Does she (live, lives) in London?

다음 괄호 안에서 알맞은 말을 골라 동그라미 하세요.

1 I (doesn't, don't) like onions.

2 Mary (doesn't, don't) say anything.

3 He (doesn't, don't) buy many shoes.

4 We (don't, doesn't) want food.

5 Mr. White (don't, doesn't) eat sugar.

6 They (don't, doesn't) play computer games.

7 Mr. Johns (don't, doesn't) watch TV.

8 Tom and Amy (don't, doesn't) walk to school.

9 The cat (doesn't, don't) run away.

10 Ms. Nora (don't, doesn't) teach English.

11 My daughters (don't, doesn't) get up early.

12 Judy and I (don't, doesn't) have breakfast.

13 The woman (don't, doesn't) eat meat.

14 Tom and you (doesn't, don't) talk about it.

15 Amy (doesn't, don't) do the dishes.

16 The men (doesn't, don't) take a taxi.

onion 양파
shoes 신발
run away 도망가다
early 일찍
taxi 택시

다음 괄호 안에서 알맞은 말을 골라 동그라미 하세요.

1 (Do, Does) you (meets, meet) Amy?

2 (Do, Does) she (arrives, arrive) on time?

3 (Do, Does) he (does, do) the dishes?

4 (Do, Does) you (drive, drives) a bus?

5 (Do, Does) I (look, looks) sad?

6 (Do, Does) the bird (sing, sings) in the tree?

7 (Do, Does) they (read, reads) books every night?

8 (Do, Does) Mary and you (have, has) lunch together?

9 (Do, Does) Matt (live, lives) in Seoul?

10 (Do, Does) the eagle (fly, flies) high in the sky?

11 (Do, Does) her son (chooses, choose) a bag?

12 (Do, Does) Jinsu and Bora (starts, start) at eight?

13 (Do, Does) Mrs. Brown (come, comes) late?

14 (Do, Does) the men (pays, pay) every time?

15 (Do, Does) she (stands, stand) at the gate?

16 (Do, Does) the boy (likes, like) grapes?

on time 정각에
dish 그릇, 접시
pay 지불하다, 돈을 내다
gate 문, 출입문

다음 괄호 안에서 알맞은 말을 골라 동그라미 하세요.

apartment 아파트
insect 곤충
heavy 무거운
luggage 짐

1 I have a sister.
He has a sister, (either, too).

2 We don't drink coffee.
They don't drink coffee, (either, too).

3 This book isn't very difficult.
That book isn't very difficult, (either, too).

4 He doesn't know its name.
She doesn't know its name, (too, either).

5 Jessica lives in an apartment.
Tim lives in an apartment, (too, either).

6 My brother studies hard.
My sister studies hard, (too, either).

7 She doesn't have a car.
He doesn't have a car, (too, either).

8 A butterfly is an insect.
An ant is an insect, (either, too).

9 We don't go to school on Sundays.
They don't go to school on Sundays, (either, too).

10 Ann carries the heavy luggage.
Sue carries the heavy luggage, (either, too).

다음 문장을 지시대로 바꿀 때, 빈칸에 알맞은 말을 쓰세요.

1 I tell a lie to my parents.

(부정문) I _____ _____ a lie to my parents.

2 She enters the room.

(의문문) _____ she _____ the room?

3 It belongs to John.

(부정문) It _____ _____ to John.

4 The movie starts at seven.

(부정문) The movie _____ _____ at seven.

5 He looks at the time table.

(의문문) _____ he _____ at the time table?

6 Jack and I ride bikes.

(부정문) Jack and I _____ _____ bikes.

7 The student asks a question.

(부정문) The student _____ _____ a question.

8 They chat with their friends.

(의문문) _____ they _____ with their friends?

9 She cleans the desk.

(의문문) _____ she _____ the desk?

10 Tony and Mark meet the guests.

(부정문) Tony and Mark _____ _____ the guests.

tell a lie 거짓말하다
belong 속하다
time table 시간표
chat 수다 떨다
guest 손님

다음 주어진 단어들을 바르게 배열하여 문장을 만드세요.

miss 놓치다
remember 기억하다

1 you / do / early / come / ?

→ _____

너는 일찍 오니?

2 play / does / he / the piano / ?

→ _____

그가 피아노를 치니?

3 she / the sky / look at / doesn't /.

→ _____

그녀는 하늘을 보지 않는다.

4 meet / they / at the bus stop / do / ?

→ _____

그들은 버스정거장에서 만나니?

5 the train / Jenny / miss / doesn't / .

→ _____

Jenny는 기차를 놓치지 않는다.

6 rain / it / does / in London / ?

→ _____

런던에는 비가 오니?

7 remember / I / his phone number / don't / .

→ _____

난 그의 전화번호를 기억하지 못한다.

8 her homework / Jane / do / does / ?

→ _____

Jane은 숙제를 하니?

다음 질문에 긍정은 Yes를, 부정은 No를 사용하여 대답을 쓰세요.

truth 사실, 진실
noise 소음
bark 짖다
build 짓다, 세우다
rose 장미

1   Does he wait for us? (긍정) → _____

2   Does she run fast? (부정) → _____

3   Does the woman carry a box? (부정) → _____

4   Do you tell the truth? (긍정) → _____

5   Does your mom bake cookies? (부정) → _____

6   Do I make a noise? (긍정) → _____

7   Does Billy have many friends? (부정) → _____

8   Does the bird sing now? (긍정) → _____

9   Do they have sandwiches? (긍정) → _____

10   Does she believe that story? (긍정) → _____

11   Do the dogs bark a lot? (부정) → _____

12   Does Mr. Park build the house? (부정) → _____

13   Do Matt and his wife stay here? (긍정) → _____

14   Does Jack play soccer? (긍정) → _____

15   Do Joe and Dan live together? (부정) → _____

16   Does she plant many roses? (긍정) → _____

다음 문장의 의문문과 부정문을 완성하세요.

address 주소
Internet 인터넷
grocery 식료품
wear 입다

1 You know her address.

(의문문) _____ her address?

(부정문) _____ her address.

2 She speaks English well.

(의문문) _____ English well?

(부정문) _____ English well.

3 They drink tea in the living room.

(의문문) _____ tea in the living room?

(부정문) _____ tea in the living room.

4 Emily gets up late.

(의문문) _____ up late?

(부정문) _____ up late.

5 They use the Internet.

(의문문) _____ the Internet?

(부정문) _____ the Internet.

6 The taxi stop there.

(의문문) _____ there?

(부정문) _____ there.

7 Sarah buys groceries here.

(의문문) _____ groceries here?

(부정문) _____ groceries here.

8 The girls wear skirts.

(의문문) _____ skirts?

(부정문) _____ skirts.

다음 문장의 빈칸에 too나 either를 쓰세요.

tomato 토마토
glasses 안경
receive 받다

1 Her children don't eat tomatoes.
   My children don't eat tomatoes, _____.

2 I buy an expensive ring.
   He buys an expensive ring, _____.

3 Jane wears glasses.
   Mary wears glasses, _____.

4 The Chinese restaurant doesn't open today.
   The Italian restaurant doesn't open today, _____.

5 They spend a lot of money.
   We spend a lot of money, _____.

6 I receive his e-mail.
   She receives his e-mail, _____.

7 They aren't busy now.
   I am not busy now, _____.

8 Her cousin doesn't leave this city.
   Her parents don't leave this city, _____.

9 His father works at a post office.
   His uncle works at a post office, _____.

10 Paul doesn't want an MP3 player.
    Jack doesn't want an MP3 player, _____.

다음 문장을 지시대로 바꾸고, 의문문의 경우 대답도 쓰세요.

lesson 수업, 레슨
alone 혼자
shower 샤워
cross 건너다
voice 목소리

1 I take a piano lesson every day.

(부정문) _____

2 Peter stays home alone.

(의문문) _____ – No, _____

3 Tom and Tony have many friends.

(부정문) _____

4 She does her homework.

(부정문) _____

5 The concert starts on time.

(의문문) _____ – Yes, _____

6 The kids swim in the pool.

(의문문) _____ – No, _____

7 The man takes a shower.

(의문문) _____ – Yes, _____

8 The woman crosses the street.

(부정문) _____

9 Judy calls her mother.

(의문문) _____ – No, _____

10 You hear my voice.

(의문문) _____ – No, _____

다음 빈칸에 알맞은 말을 쓰세요.

Ⅰ 일반동사의 부정문

• 일반동사 문장의 부정문은 _____ 앞에 _____ 나 _____ 를 붙여 만든다.

	단수	do(es)+not	일반동사	복수	do(es)+not	일반동사
1인칭	I	_____		We		
2인칭	You	don't	동사원형 ~.	You	_____	동사원형 ~.
3인칭	He She It	_____		They		

2 일반동사의 의문문

• **일반동사 의문문:** _____ 앞에 _____ 나 _____ 를 붙이고 문장 맨 뒤에 _____ 를 붙여 의문 문을 만든다. 뒤에 오는 일반동사는 -s나 -es가 붙지 않은 _____ 의 형태로 쓴다.

• **대답하기:** 대답이 긍정이면 _____ 를, 부정이면 _____ 를 사용하여 답한다.

• 의문문의 주어가 _____ , 2인칭일 때는 대답의 주어가 달라진다.

의문문	긍정의 대답	부정의 대답
Do I ~? 내가 ~하니?	Yes, _____ do.	No, _____ don't.
Do we ~? 우리가 ~하니?	Yes, you[_____] do.	No, you[_____] don't.
Do you ~? 너는 ~하니?	Yes, I do.	No, I don't.
Do you ~? 너희는 ~하니?	Yes, _____ do.	No, _____ don't.
Does he/she ~? 그/그녀는 ~하니?	Yes, he/she does.	Yes, he/she _____.

3 긍정문 또는 부정문에서의 '~도, 또한'

'~도, 또한' 이라는 뜻으로 긍정문에는 _____ 를 부정문에서는 _____ 를 사용한다.

주어진 말을 사용하여 부정문 또는 의문문 문장을 완성하세요.

1 _____ math class today? (have, you, 의문문)

2 _____ the radio. (listen to, Paul, 부정문)

3 _____ a school uniform? (wear, she, 의문문)

4 _____ to church? (they, go, 의문문)

5 _____ my house. (that, be동사, 부정문)

6 _____ it. (my son, remember, 부정문)

7 _____ from England? (you, be동사, 의문문)

8 _____ his mother? (John, call, 의문문)

9 _____ a horse. (my friend, ride, 부정문)

10 _____ the phone? (you, use, 의문문)

11 _____ at Ann. (they, laugh, 부정문)

12 _____ late for school? (he, be동사, 의문문)

13 _____ at five? (the party, begin, 의문문)

14 _____ near here? (live, your sisters, 의문문)

15 _____ at the airport. (arrive, Henry, 부정문)

16 _____ heavy. (be동사, the books, 부정문)

school uniform
교복

church 교회

call 전화하다

airport 공항

다음 문장을 지시대로 바꾸고, 의문문의 경우 대답도 완성하세요.

meal 식사
cook 요리사
diary 일기
photo 사진

1 They come from China.

(의문문) _____ – Yes, _____

2 Mr. Brown writes letters.

(의문문) _____ – No, _____

3 We go to school on Sundays.

(부정문) _____

4 She knows Mr. Park.

(부정문) _____

5 You do the dishes after meals.

(의문문) _____ – Yes, _____

6 Mr. Baker is a cook.

(부정문) _____

7 Your daughter has a doll.

(의문문) _____ – No, _____

8 Your grandmother reads a book.

(부정문) _____

9 Suji keeps a diary every day.

(의문문) _____ – Yes, _____

10 These are your photos.

(의문문) _____ – Yes, _____

다음 문장의 밑줄 친 부분을 바르게 고쳐 빈칸에 쓰세요.

enter 들어가다
restaurant 음식점
health 건강
ring 울리다

1 <u>Do</u> he fly the kite? → _____

2 Mrs. Kim <u>doesn't enters</u> the house. → _____

3 <u>Is he play</u> the guitar? → _____

4 <u>Does</u> Tim and Ava live in Seoul? → _____

5 They <u>have not</u> their room. → _____

6 Does Sue <u>meets</u> him in the restaurant? → _____

7 She and I <u>not wait</u> for friends. → _____

8 <u>Are you worry</u> about the health? → _____

9 Does Jim like apples? – No, <u>he does</u>. → _____

10 Paul <u>don't see</u> many people in the city. → _____

11 Does Cathy <u>travels</u> in France? → _____

12 <u>Does</u> you believe the news? → _____

13 I don't have brothers.
    She doesn't have brothers, <u>too</u>. → _____

14 <u>Are your sister buy</u> flowers? → _____

15 My dad <u>don't washes</u> his car. → _____

16 The man <u>doesn't rings</u> the bell. → _____

1 다음 중 don't가 들어가기에 알맞은 곳을 고르세요.

They ① eat ② dinner ③ at
④ seven o'clock.

[2~4] 다음 문장의 빈칸에 알맞은 말을 고르세요.

2
> She _____ need a new jacket.
> 그녀는 새 재킷이 필요하지 않다.

① isn't   ② aren't
③ don't   ④ doesn't

3
> Mr. Han _____ teach science.
> 한 선생님은 과학을 가르치지 않는다.

① isn't   ② aren't
③ don't   ④ doesn't

4
> Sam and Judy _____ go to the city.
> Sam과 Judy는 그 도시로 가지 않는다.

① isn't   ② aren't
③ don't   ④ doesn't

[5~6] 다음 중 바르지 않은 문장을 고르세요.

5
① They don't use the Internet.
② You aren't win the game.
③ She doesn't cook dinner.
④ We don't take a taxi.

6
① Do you run fast?
② Does the shop open today?
③ Does your father sells cars?
④ Do Brian's sons play soccer?

7 다음 빈칸에 공통으로 알맞은 말을 고르세요.

> A: _____ Amy ride a bicycle?
> B: Yes, she _____.

① do   ② don't
③ does   ④ doesn't

[8~10] 다음 의문문에 대한 대답으로 알맞은 것을 고르세요.

8 Do you know his phone number?
① Yes, I do.   ② Yes, I don't.
③ No, you do.   ④ No, you don't.

9 Does Annie call you?
① Yes, you does.
② Yes, she doesn't.
③ No, she doesn't.
④ No, they don't.

10 Do your brothers read comic books?
① Yes, he does.
② Yes, they do.
③ No, they doesn't.
④ No, it doesn't.

11 다음 중 빈칸에 들어갈 말이 <u>다른</u> 것을 고르세요.

① _____ she write letters?

② _____ he play basketball?

③ _____ Mrs. Kim wait for a bus?

④ _____ your mom a school teacher?

12 다음 문장을 의문문으로 바꿔 쓰세요.

The students wear school uniforms.

→ _____

13 다음 중 빈칸에 들어갈 말이 <u>다른</u> 것은?

① I take a rest. She takes a rest, _____.

② A lion runs fast. A horse runs fast, _____.

③ She is a cook. Her sister is a cook, _____.

④ He doesn't answer. His son doesn't answer, _____.

[14~15] 다음 대화의 빈칸에 알맞은 말을 고르세요.

14
> A: Does Judy wear sunglasses?
> B: _____. She wear a cap.

① Yes, she is.

② No, she isn't.

③ Yes, she does.

④ No, she doesn't.

15
> A: Do the children use the computer?
> B: _____ They play computer games.

① Yes, he do.　② No, she doesn't.

③ Yes, they do.　④ No, they don't.

16 다음 주어진 문장을 부정문과 의문문으로 고쳐 쓰세요.

Your friends study at the library.

(부정문) → _____

(의문문) → _____

[17~18] 다음에서 틀린 부분을 찾아 ○표 하고, 문장을 고쳐 다시 쓰세요.

17 Does Henry exercises every day?

→ _____

18 They aren't arrive at school.

→ _____

[19~20] 다음 우리말과 같도록 주어진 단어를 사용하여 문장을 완성하세요.

19 파티는 8시에 시작하니? (begin)

→ _____ at eight o'clock?

20 그녀는 식사 후에 설거지를 하지 않는다. (do)

→ _____ the dishes after meals.

A 다음 우리말을 참고하여 가족을 소개하는 글을 완성하세요.

Let me introduce my family. My dad is a teacher. _____ _____ his students. My mom is a housewife. She _____ _____ well. I have two sisters. They _____ students. They like books. They _____ _____ TV. I _____ watch TV, _____. I _____ _____ a brother. I have a cat, Pit. I love Pit.

가족을 소개할게. 아빠는 교사야. 그는 학생들을 사랑해. 엄마는 가정주부야. 그녀는 요리를 잘하지 않아. 나는 두 여자 형제가 있어. 그들은 학생이야. 그들은 책을 좋아해. 그들은 TV를 보지 않아. 나도 또한 TV를 보지 않아. 나는 남자 형제가 없어. 나는 고양이 Pit이 있어. 나는 Pit을 사랑해.

B 다음 그림을 보고, 대화의 빈칸에 알맞은 말을 쓰세요.

A: _____ you want coffee?

B: No, I _____. I want orange juice.

A: OK. _____ your son want orange juice, too?

B: Yes, he does.

There is/are ~, 비인칭 주어 it

There is/are ~ 구문의 긍정문을 이해하고 활용할 수 있다.

There is/are ~ 구문의 부정문을 이해하고 활용할 수 있다.

There is/are ~ 구문의 의문문을 이해하고 활용할 수 있다.

비인칭 주어 it의 쓰임을 이해하고 활용할 수 있다.

There is ~, There are ~ 구문에서는 be동사가 '~이 있다'라는 뜻이에요.

There는 '거기에'라는 뜻이 있지만, 이 경우에는 해석하지 않아요.

시간, 날씨, 요일, 거리 등을 나타낼 때, 주어로 it을 쓰는데, 이때의 it을 비인칭 주어라고 하며 비인칭 주어 it은 '그것'이라고 해석하지 않아요.

Unit 3
There is/are ~, 비인칭 주어 it

1. There is, There are ~ 문장

There is/are ~ 문장에서 주어는 be동사 뒤에 위치하며 '~이 있다'라는 뜻이다. There는 단순히 문장을 유도하기 위한 부사로, 해석하지 않는다.

• There is 다음에는 단수 주어가 오고, There are 다음에는 복수 주어가 온다.

| There is | + | 단수 주어 | = ~이 있다 |

| There are | + | 복수 주어 | = ~들이 있다 |

There is a book in the box. 상자 안에 책이 한 권 있다.

There are two books in the box. 상자 안에 책이 두 권 있다.

• 고유명사나 물질명사처럼 셀 수 없는 명사는 단수 주어임에 유의한다. 단, 물질명사의 경우 단위명사를 이용해 셀 수 있다.

There is milk in the bottle. 그 병 안에 우유가 있다.

There are three glasses of milk on the table. 탁자 위에 우유 석 잔이 있다.

2. There is, There are ~ 부정문

부정문은 be동사 뒤에 not을 붙여 '~이 있지 않다/없다'를 표현한다.

There is not[isn't] a ball in the box. 상자 안에 공이 한 개도 없다.

There are not[aren't] balls in the box. 상자 안에 공들이 없다.

3. There is, There are ~ 의문문

의문문은 be동사를 there 앞으로 보내고 문장 끝에 물음표(?)를 붙여 '~이 있니?'라고 묻는 말을 나타낸다.

• 대답은 긍정이면 Yes, 부정이면 No로 한다.

There is a ball in the box.

Is there a ball in the box? 상자 안에 공이 한 개 있니?

– Yes, there is. 응, 있어. / No, there isn't. 아니, 없어.

There are many balls in the box.

Are there many balls in the box? 상자 안에 많은 공이 있니?

– Yes, there are. 응, 있어. / No, there aren't. 아니, 없어.

> **Pop Quiz**
> 1. 다음 괄호 안에서 알맞은 것을 고르세요.
> ❶ There (am, is, are) an apple on the table.
> ❷ There (am, is, are) three chairs in the room.

4. 비인칭 주어 it

it은 시간, 요일, 날짜, 날씨 등을 나타낼 때 주어로 쓰는데, 이때의 it을 비인칭 주어라 한다. 비인칭 주어 it은 '그것'이라고 해석하지 않는다.

① 시간, 요일, 날짜 등을 나타낼 때

What time is it? 몇 시인가요?   – It's nine o'clock. 9시입니다.

What day is it? 무슨 요일인가요?   – It's Monday. 월요일입니다.

What date is it? 날짜가 며칠인가요? – It's May 1st. 5월 1일입니다.

How long does it take to Seoul? 서울까지 얼마나 걸리나요?

– It takes one hour. 1시간 걸려요.

② 날씨를 나타낼 때

How's the weather?   – It's cloudy. 흐려요.

   – It's cold. 추워요.

③ 명암을 나타낼 때

It's dark. 어두워요.   It's bright. 밝아요.

It＋동사	시간, 요일, 날짜, 날씨, 명암, 거리를 나타내는 말

5. 비인칭 주어 it vs 대명사 it

• 비인칭 주어 it: 아무런 뜻 없이 주어로 '시간, 날씨, 날짜, 요일, 거리, 명암' 등을 나타낼 때 사용된다.

It's raining. 비가 오는 중이다. [비인칭 주어]

• 대명사 it: 앞에 나온 명사를 대신해서, '그것'이라는 뜻으로 사용된다.

I have an umbrella. It is yellow. 우산이 있다. 그것은 노란색이다. [대명사]

Pop Quiz   2. 다음 괄호 안에서 알맞은 것을 고르세요.

❶ (It, There) is snowing.   ❷ (It, There) is Tuesday.

다음 괄호 안에서 알맞은 말을 골라 동그라미 하세요.

1 There (is, are) an eraser in the pencil case.

2 There (is, are) four clerks in the store.

3 There (is, are) a cat on the sofa.

4 There (is, are) some flour in the bowl.

5 There (is, are) many mountains in Japan.

6 There (is, are) a printer between the computers.

7 There (is, are) an oven in the dining room.

8 There (is, are) three pillows on the bed.

9 There (is, are) food in the refrigerator.

10 There (is, are) a bicycle in the yard.

11 There (is, are) many people at the station.

12 There (is, are) students in the library.

13 There (is, are) a lot of milk in the cup.

14 There (is, are) two boys in the pool.

15 There (is, are) a taxi in front of my house.

16 There (is, are) some bees among the flowers.

clerk 점원
printer 프린터기
between ~ 사이에
oven 오븐
pillow 베개
refrigerator 냉장고
among ~ 사이에

다음 빈칸에 There is와 There are 중에서 알맞은 말을 쓰세요.

garden 정원
plate 접시
soup 수프
coin 동전
pocket 주머니

1 _____ a mirror on the wall.

2 _____ many trees in the park.

3 _____ a camera on the desk.

4 _____ some juice in the glass.

5 _____ three cups of coffee on the table.

6 _____ a lot of flowers in the garden.

7 _____ a pretty girl among the boys.

8 _____ little food on the plate.

9 _____ eleven tables in the restaurant.

10 _____ some soup in the bowl.

11 _____ 300 students in our school.

12 _____ a dog under the tree.

13 _____ a fork beside the plate.

14 _____ two children in the school bus.

15 _____ three coins in my pocket.

16 _____ some tea in the cup.

다음 우리말과 같도록 괄호 안에서 알맞은 말을 고르세요.

island 섬
beside 옆에

1 토요일이다.

= (It, There) is Saturday.

2 나는 야구 모자가 하나 있다. 그것은 갈색이다.

= I have a cap. (It, There) is brown.

3 제주도까지 비행기로 1시간 걸린다.

= (It, There) takes an hour to Jeju island by plane.

4 늦었어. 지금 9시야.

= I'm late. (It, This) is nine o'clock now.

5 춥다. 재킷을 입어라.

= (It, There) is cold. Put on your jacket.

6 그 여자 옆에 한 남자가 있다.

= (There, It) is a man beside the woman.

7 4월 1일이다.

= (There, It) is April 1st.

8 전등을 켜. 어두워.

= Turn on the light. (There, It) is dark.

9 창 밖을 봐! 눈이 와.

= Look out of the window! (It, There) is snowing.

10 너를 위한 선물이 있어. 그것은 내 가방 안에 있어.

= I have a gift for you. (There, It) is in my bag.

다음 괄호 안에서 알맞은 말을 골라 동그라미 하세요.

a bunch of
한 다발, 한 묶음
kitten 새끼 고양이
hole 구멍
moon 달

1   There is (a lady, some ladies) next to him.

2   There are (a picture, pictures) on the wall.

3   There is (flowers, a bunch of flowers) in the vase.

4   There are (7 day, 7 days) in a week.

5   There is (a park, five parks) in the town.

6   There is (a kitten, some kittens) in my house.

7   There is (a lot of trees, a lot of snow) on the street.

8   There is (an ant, some ants) near the hole.

9   There are (Mr. White, Mr. and Mrs. White) at the shop.

10   There are (five Monday, five Mondays) in July.

11   There is (some sugar, some candies) in the paper bag.

12   There is (a moon, many stars) in the sky.

13   There are (many fish, a fish) in the pond.

14   There is (a little flour, two cups of flour) in the bowl.

15   There are (12 month, 12 months) in a year.

16   There is (a cute puppy, cute puppies) in the garden.

다음 문장의 의문문과 부정문을 완성하세요.

tulip 튤립
storage 창고
pet shop
애완동물 가게

1 There are five baseball teams in the city.
(의문문) _____ five baseball teams in the city?
(부정문) _____ five baseball teams in the city.

2 There is a butterfly among the tulips.
(의문문) _____ a butterfly among the tulips?
(부정문) _____ a butterfly among the tulips.

3 There are two rings in his hand.
(의문문) _____ two rings in his hand?
(부정문) _____ two rings in his hand.

4 There is a lot of rice in the storage.
(의문문) _____ a lot of rice in the storage?
(부정문) _____ a lot of rice in the storage.

5 There are twelve teachers in this school.
(의문문) _____ twelve teachers in this school?
(부정문) _____ twelve teachers in this school.

6 There are ten people in the park.
(의문문) _____ ten people in the park?
(부정문) _____ ten people in the park.

7 There are five dogs in the pet shop.
(의문문) _____ five dogs in the pet shop?
(부정문) _____ five dogs in the pet shop.

8 There is a bank near my house.
(의문문) _____ a bank near my house?
(부정문) _____ a bank near my house.

다음 질문에 Yes와 No의 대답을 쓰세요. (부정은 축약형으로 쓸 것)

university 대학

1 Are there 15 players in this soccer team?

Yes, _____.

No, _____.

2 Are there 365 days in a year?

Yes, _____.

No, _____.

3 Are there many universities in Korea?

Yes, _____.

No, _____.

4 Is there a doctor in the plane?

Yes, _____.

No, _____.

5 Are there a lot of animals in the zoo?

Yes, _____.

No, _____.

6 Is there a dog in front of Sam?

Yes, _____.

No, _____.

7 Is there a guitar in his room?

Yes, _____.

No, _____.

8 Are there a few toys in the market?

Yes, _____.

No, _____.

다음 빈칸에 '~(들)이 있다'라는 뜻이 되도록 알맞은 말을 쓰세요.

piece 조각
sheet 장

1 _____ a television in the classroom.

2 _____ two pieces of cake on the plate.

3 _____ three balls in my bag.

4 _____ a laptop in his car.

5 _____ three loaves of bread in the basket.

6 _____ a child beside the man.

7 _____ Sam and Jina in the bus.

8 _____ hot water in the glass.

9 _____ some tea in the cup.

10 _____ a lot of doctors in the hospital.

11 _____ a bee among the flowers.

12 _____ eleven players in the soccer team.

13 _____ a ruler in the pencil case.

14 _____ six sheets of paper on the desk.

15 _____ a lot of plants in her garden.

16 _____ a big painting on the wall.

다음 우리말과 같도록 빈칸에 알맞은 말을 쓰세요.

country 시골, 나라
comb 빗
little 거의 없는

1 이 방 안에 모기가 몇 마리 있다.

= _____ ____ a few mosquitoes in this room.

2 나는 집이 하나 있다. 그것은 시골에 있다.

= I have a house. _____ ____ in the country.

3 부산까지 기차로 3시간이 걸린다.

= ____ _____ three hours to Busan by train.

4 서둘러라. 4시야.

= Hurry up. _____ ____ four o'clock.

5 탁자 위에 빗이 한 자루 있다.

= _____ ____ a comb on the table.

6 그 소년 옆에 큰 고양이가 한 마리 있다.

= _____ ____ a big cat beside the boy.

7 생일 축하해. 7월 5일이야.

= Happy birthday! ____ ____ July 5th.

8 그 식당에는 6명의 웨이터가 있다.

= _____ ____ six waiters in the restaurant.

9 우산을 가지고 가. 비가 와.

= Take your umbrella with you. ____ ____ raining.

10 창고 안에 음식이 거의 없다.

= _____ ____ little food in the storage.

다음 문장의 의문문과 부정문을 쓰세요.

1 There is a soccer team in the city.

(의문문) _____

(부정문) _____

2 There are bees on the flowers.

(의문문) _____

(부정문) _____

3 There is a lot of flour in the paper bag.

(의문문) _____

(부정문) _____

4 There is little rice in the plastic bag.

(의문문) _____

(부정문) _____

5 There are foreign teachers in this school.

(의문문) _____

(부정문) _____

6 There are a lot of people in the gym.

(의문문) _____

(부정문) _____

7 There are few kittens in the pet shop.

(의문문) _____

(부정문) _____

8 There is a library between the bank and the hospital.

(의문문) _____

(부정문) _____

plastic 플라스틱

foreign
외국의, 외국인의

gym 체육관

다음 빈칸에 알맞은 말을 쓰세요.

┃ There is, There are ~ 긍정문

- There is/are ~ 구문에서는 주어는 be동사 뒤에 위치한다. _____는 '~이 있다' 라는 뜻이다.

- 고유명사나 물질명사처럼 _____ 명사는 단수 주어임에 유의한다. 단, 물질명사의 경우 단위 명사를 이용해 셀 수 있다.

$$\boxed{\text{There \_\_\_\_}} \; + \; \boxed{\text{단수 주어}} \; = \text{~이 있다}$$

$$\boxed{\text{There \_\_\_\_}} \; + \; \boxed{\text{복수 주어}} \; = \text{~들이 있다}$$

2 There is, There are ~ 부정문

- be동사 뒤에 _____을 붙여 '~이 있지 않다/없다'를 표현한다.

3 There is, There are ~ 의문문

- be동사를 _____ 앞으로 보내고 문장 끝에 _____를 붙여 '~이 있니?'라고 묻는 말을 나타낸다.

- 대답은 긍정이면 _____, 부정이면 _____로 한다.

4 비인칭 주어 it

- _____은 보통 앞에 나온 명사를 대신해서 '_____'이라는 뜻의 대명사로 쓰인다. 아무런 뜻 없이 시간이나 날씨, 명암, 거리 등을 표현할 때 비인칭 주어 _____을 쓴다.

다음 문장을 There로 시작하는 문장으로 바꿔 쓰세요.

behind ~ 뒤에
cage 우리
bottle 병
shelf 선반

1   A chair is beside the sofa.

_____

2   Tom and his sister are in the classroom.

_____

3   A white table is in my house.

_____

4   Many rivers are in Korea.

_____

5   A bank is behind the building.

_____

6   Six pieces of pizza are on the table.

_____

7   Some oranges are in the basket.

_____

8   A small fox is in the cage.

_____

9   Three bottles of juice are on the shelf.

_____

10 A lot of cheese is in the storage.

_____

다음 문장에서 틀린 부분을 바르게 고쳐 다시 쓰세요.

difficult 어려운
furniture 가구

1 There are a little milk in the glass.

_____

2 There is four Chinese restaurants in this town.

_____

3 Is there many people in the park?

_____

4 There isn't difficult problems in the exam.

_____

5 There are one man in the gym.

_____

6 There are not a lot of rain in summer.

_____

7 There is five bunches of grapes in the basket.

_____

8 Take an umbrella. This is raining.

_____

9 Are there some pepper in the jar?

_____

10 There is four pieces of furniture in the room.

_____

Jump Up 4

다음에서 틀린 부분을 고쳐 다시 쓰고, 의문문은 대답도 완성하세요.

plant 식물
flower shop 꽃가게
season 계절

1 There is many plants at the flower shop.

_____

2 Is there many fish under the sea?

_____ Yes, _____

3 Is there some papers on the desk?

_____ No, _____

4 That takes two hours to Jeju island.

_____

5 There are not some flour in the paper bag.

_____

6 Is there a lot of people in the office?

_____ No, _____

7 There is four seasons in Korea.

_____

8 Is there three math classes in a week?

_____ Yes, _____

9 Get up. This is nine o'clock now.

_____

10 Is there some old women in the museum?

_____ Yes, _____

[1~3] 다음 문장의 빈칸에 알맞은 말을 고르세요.

1 There is _____ on the table.
① some cheese ② apples
③ a few dishes ④ forks

2 There are _____ in the school.
① a foreign teacher ② a gym
③ a small pond ④ students

3 Is there _____ in this zoo?
① many animals ② lions
③ an elephant ④ monkeys

[4~5] 다음 대화의 빈칸에 들어갈 말을 고르세요.

4
A: Is there food in the refrigerator?
B: _____

① Yes, it is. ② No, it isn't.
③ Yes, there is. ④ There isn't.

5
A: Are there any Italian restaurants here?
B: _____

① There are.
② Yes, they are.
③ No, they aren't.
④ No, there aren't.

6 다음 중 not이 들어가기에 알맞은 곳을 고르세요.
There ① is ② a piece of ③ furniture ④ in the room.

[7~8] 다음 빈칸에 들어갈 말을 고르세요.

7 There _____ some juice in the jar.
① am ② are
③ is ④ has

8 There _____ a lot of problems in the city.
① am ② are
③ is ④ has

9 다음 두 문장이 같은 뜻이 되도록 빈칸에 알맞은 말을 고르세요.

Six windows are in the house.
= There _____ six windows in the house.

① is ② are
③ has ④ have

10 밑줄 친 it의 쓰임이 다른 것은?
① It's 7:30.
② It is sunny.
③ I have a bicycle. It is blue.
④ Turn on the light. It's dark.

11 다음 문장을 부정문으로 바꾸어 쓰시오.

There is a bank next to the library.

→ _____

12 다음 문장을 의문문으로 바꾸어 쓰시오.

There is a bus stop around here.

→ _____

13 다음 중 빈칸에 들어갈 말이 <u>다른</u> 것을 고르세요.

① _____ is snowing.
② _____ is June 5th.
③ _____ is far from here.
④ _____ is some water in the cup.

[14~15] 다음 중 빈칸에 들어갈 말을 고르세요.

14 There is _____ on the dish.

① some sugar
② some pieces of cake
③ two pieces of
④ some cakes

15 There are _____ on the desk.

① a glass of milk
② two books
③ some paper
④ a computer

16 다음 우리말에 맞도록 주어진 단어를 배열하여 문장을 쓰세요.

> 그 탁자 위에 커피 석 잔이 있니?
> (coffee, on, are, three cups of, there, the table, ?)

_____

[17~18] 다음 대화의 빈칸에 알맞은 말을 고르세요.

17
> A: Is it raining?
> B: _____ It's sunny.

① Yes, it is.　　② No, it isn't.
③ Yes, it does.　④ No, it doesn't.

18
> A: Is there a market around here?
> B: _____. It is across the street.

① Yes, it is.　　② No, it isn't.
③ Yes, there is.　④ No, there isn't.

[19~20] 다음 문장에서 <u>틀린</u> 곳을 바르게 고쳐 다시 쓰세요.

19 There is some singers on the stage.

_____

20 Hurry up. They are eleven o'clock.

_____

A 다음 그림을 묘사하는 글을 완성하세요.

It's sunny. _____ _____ many animals in the zoo. There is an elephant. _____ is big. _____ _____ three giraffes. _____ are tall. There are _____ monkeys in the tree. They have bananas. There is a sheep. _____ _____ a man beside the sheep. There are _____ any lions in the zoo.

B 다음 그림을 보고, 대화의 빈칸에 알맞은 말을 쓰세요.

A: Is there a library in this town?

B: No, _____ _____.

A: _____ there a bookstore?

B: _____, _____ _____.
   It's between the bank and the school.

A: Thank you.

Unit 4

형용사

형용사의 종류와 쓰임을 이해하고 활용할 수 있다.

형용사를 알맞은 위치에 사용할 수 있다.

형용사는 바로 명사 앞에서 명사를 꾸며 주거나, be동사와 함께 쓰여 주어를 보충 설명 해 주는 역할을 해요. 또한 형용사에는 지시형용사, 수량형용사, 성질을 나타내는 형용 사가 있어요.

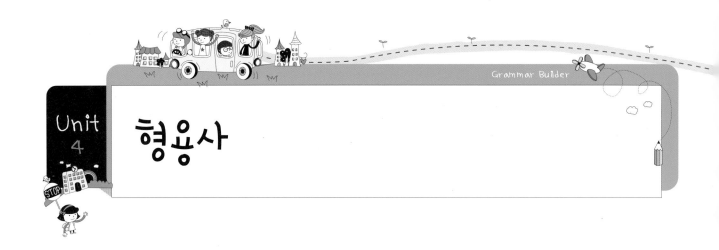

Unit 4

형용사

1. 형용사의 의미와 종류

형용사란 명사를 꾸며 주거나 설명해 주는 말로, '~한'이라는 의미이다.

• 형용사에는 지시형용사, 수량형용사, 성질을 나타내는 형용사가 있다.

지시형용사	this, that, these, those
수량형용사	one, two, three, many, much, a lot of ...
성질형용사	상태, 색깔, 날씨, 맛 등을 나타내는 beautiful, red, cold, sweet

• 성질형용사의 종류

종류	단어
상태	big 큰, clever 영리한, fast 빠른, full 배부른, great 훌륭한, handsome 잘생긴, new 새로운, nice 멋진, pretty 예쁜
색깔	red 빨간, orange 주황색의, yellow 노란, green 초록색의, blue 파란, navy 남색의, violet 보라색의, white 흰색의
날씨	cool 시원한, cloudy 흐린, hot 더운, rainy 비가 오는, snowy 눈이 오는, cloudy 구름이 낀, sunny 화창한, warm 따뜻한, windy 바람이 부는
맛	bitter 쓴, hot 매운, salty 짠, sour 신, sweet 달콤한

명사에 -y나 -ly를 붙여서 형용사를 만들 수도 있다.
cloud - cloudy 구름이 낀, wind - windy 바람이 부는,
rain - rainy 비가 내리는, salt - salty 짠맛이 나는
love - lovely 사랑스런, friend - friendly 친한,
luck - lucky 행운의

2. 형용사의 쓰임 (1)

형용사는 명사 바로 앞에 와서 명사를 꾸며 주는데, 이를 형용사의 '한정적 용법'이라고 한다.

This is a beautiful park. 이것은 아름다운 공원이다.
   형용사   명사

I know a tall boy. 나는 키가 큰 소년을 안다.
   형용사 명사

Pop Quiz   Ⅰ. 다음 중 형용사를 찾아 동그라미하세요.
   ❶ (handsome, flower, boy)   ❷ (winter, friend, snowy)

3. 형용사의 쓰임 (2)

형용사는 주어를 보충 설명해 주는 역할을 한다. 이때, 형용사는 동사 뒤에 온다. 이를 형용사의 '서술적 용법'이라고 한다.

Eric is kind. Eric은 친절하다.
주어   형용사

This park is beautiful. 이 공원은 아름답다.
   주어   형용사

> 형용사의 쓰임
> 1. '형용사+명사'의 형태로 명사 앞에서 명사를 꾸며 준다.
> 2. 동사 뒤에서 주어의 성질이나 상태를 설명해 준다.

4. 형용사의 위치

형용사가 명사를 꾸며주는 경우에는 형용사의 위치에 유의해야 한다.

❶ a/an＋형용사＋명사

I know a <u>tall</u> <u>boy</u>. 나는 키가 큰 소년을 안다.
　　　　　형용사＋명사

바로 뒤에 오는 형용사의
첫 소리에 따라 a나 an을 써야한다.
an orange, a big orange / a house, an old house

❷ a/an＋부사＋형용사＋명사

He is a <u>very</u> <u>tall</u> <u>boy</u>. 그는 아주 키가 큰 소년이다.
　　　　　부사＋형용사＋명사

❸ 소유격＋형용사＋명사

He is <u>my</u> <u>tall</u> <u>friend</u>. 그는 내 키가 큰 친구이다.
　　　　소유격＋형용사 ＋ 명사

❹ 2개 이상의 형용사가 명사를 수식하는 경우, '지시형용사＋수량형용사＋성질형용사＋명사' 순
으로 온다.

<u>These</u> <u>many</u> <u>red</u> <u>apples</u> are big. 이 많은 빨간 사과는 크다.
지시형용사 ＋ 수량형용사 ＋성질형용사 ＋ 명사

소유격이나 지시형용사와
명사가 함께 올 경우, 관사(a/an, the)는 붙지 않는다.
a my big orange (✗), a this big orange (✗)
my big orange (O), this big orange (O)

Pop Quiz **2.** 다음 괄호 안에서 알맞은 것을 고르세요.

　　❶ She is (pretty, girl).　　❷ This (green, the) jacket is mine.

다음 빈칸에 알맞은 형용사를 쓰세요.

1	젊은 young	↔ 나이든	_____
2	큰 big	↔ 작은	_____
3	키가 큰 tall	↔ 키가 작은	_____
4	깨끗한 clean	↔ 더러운	_____
5	부유한 rich	↔ 가난한	_____
6	약한 weak	↔ 강한	_____
7	배부른 full	↔ 배고픈	_____
8	뜨거운 hot	↔ 차가운	_____
9	빠른 fast	↔ 느린	_____
10	긴 long	↔ 짧은	_____
11	열린 open	↔ 닫힌	_____
12	한가한 free	↔ 바쁜	_____
13	쉬운 easy	↔ 어려운	_____
14	비싼 expensive	↔ 값싼	_____
15	젖은 wet	↔ 마른	_____
16	가벼운 light	↔ 무거운	_____

poor 가난한
closed 닫힌
difficult 어려운
cheap 값싼

다음 문장에서 형용사를 찾아 동그라미 하고 뜻을 쓰세요.

handsome 잘생긴
cool 멋진, 시원한
famous 유명한
outside 밖에

1 The man is very handsome.   _____

2 It is very a cool game.   _____

3 He is a great painter.   _____

4 I am sleepy all day.   _____

5 She has famous pictures.   _____

6 The house is very big.   _____

7 The two girls are his daughters.   _____

8 Look at the old house.   _____

9 It is very a difficult test.   _____

10 There are busy men in the office.   _____

11 The sky is blue.   _____

12 The food is delicious.   _____

13 It is windy outside.   _____

14 The lovely baby is smiling.   _____

15 Your jacket is wet.   _____

16 I carry a heavy bag.   _____

다음 괄호 안의 단어를 알맞은 위치에 넣어 문장을 다시 쓰세요.

1 She is a student. (new)

→ _____

2 The boy has a puppy. (cute, very)

→ _____

3 These are books. (new, their)

→ _____

4 He brings us news. (happy, very)

→ _____

5 The boys look at these flowers. (many)

→ _____

6 Mrs. White is a teacher. (very, kind)

→ _____

7 It is a coat. (long, very)

→ _____

8 The leaves are falling. (three, brown)

→ _____

9 He is a man. (strong, very)

→ _____

10 I love her paintings. (beautiful)

→ _____

puppy 강아지
bring 가져오다
coat 코트
fall 떨어지다
painting 그림

다음 우리말과 같도록 주어진 단어를 배열하여 문장을 완성하세요.

drink 마시다
smart 영리한
useful 유용한
diligent 부지런한

1 저것은 그녀의 노란색 치마이다. (skirt, her, yellow).

→ That is _____.

2 많은 오래된 집들이 있다. (many, houses, old)

→ There are _____.

3 그는 차가운 물을 마신다. (water, cold)

→ He drinks _____.

4 그것은 너의 멋진 자동차이다. (your, very, car, nice)

→ It is _____.

5 그녀는 매우 친절한 간호사이다. (a, nurse, very, kind)

→ She is _____.

6 그것은 나의 새 우산이다. (new, umbrella, my)

→ It is _____.

7 John은 그녀의 영리한 아들이다. (her, smart, son)

→ John is _____.

8 그것들은 매우 유용한 책들이다. (useful, books, very)

→ Those are _____.

9 저 부지런한 여자는 나의 친구이다. (woman, that, diligent)

→ _____ is my friend.

10 나는 비싼 의자가 하나 있다. (an, chair, expensive)

→ I have _____.

다음 우리말을 참고하여 빈칸에 알맞은 말을 쓰세요.

1 The building _____ _____. 그 건물은 높다.

2 His sister _____ _____. 그의 여동생은 게으르다.

3 I _____ _____. 나는 춥다.

4 Apples _____ _____. 사과는 빨간색이다.

5 The door _____ _____. 그 문이 열려 있다.

6 Her sneakers _____ _____. 그녀의 운동화는 더럽다.

7 The flower shop _____ _____. 그 꽃가게는 문을 닫았다.

8 The woman _____ _____. 그 여자는 한가하다.

9 These problems _____ _____. 이 문제들은 어렵다.

10 The river _____ _____. 그 강은 깊다.

11 Your shirt _____ _____. 너의 셔츠는 파란색이다.

12 The picture _____ _____. 그 그림은 크다.

13 This house _____ _____. 이 집은 검정색이다.

14 Her daughters _____ _____. 그녀의 딸들은 아름답다.

15 That book _____ _____. 저 책은 무겁다.

16 My puppy _____ _____. 나의 강아지는 귀엽다.

high 높은
lazy 게으른
sneakers 운동화
dirty 더러운
deep 깊은

다음 주어진 단어들을 바르게 배열하여 문장을 완성하세요.

sofa 소파
actor 배우
dictionary 사전

1 happy / is / father / very / my
→ _____

2 a / has / she / small / dog / very
→ _____

3 is / a / Jim / baseball / player / good
→ _____

4 like / this / I / sofa / white
→ _____

5 those are / old / very / houses
→ _____

6 famous / very / the / actor / is
→ _____

7 very / a / dictionary / it / useful / is
→ _____

8 very / these are / sneakers / clean
→ _____

9 dirty / glasses / hers / are / these
→ _____

10 two / has / brother / my / bicycles / small
→ _____

다음 문장의 빈칸에 반대의 뜻을 가진 형용사를 이용해 완성하세요.

1 My room is not dirty.

= My room _____.

2 Your umbrella is wet.

= Your umbrella _____.

3 Those women are strong.

= Those women _____.

4 The ring is expensive.

= The ring _____.

5 The city is not dangerous.

= The city _____.

6 My father is fat.

= My father _____.

7 Jordan is lazy.

= Jordan _____.

8 The volleyball players are tall.

= The volleyball players _____.

9 The road is narrow.

= The road _____.

10 Trains are fast.

= Trains _____.

ring 반지
volleyball 배구
road 길
narrow 좁은
wide 넓은

다음 두 문장이 같도록 반대의 뜻을 가진 형용사를 이용해 완성하세요.

furniture 가구
light 가벼운, 밝은
dark 어두운
unkind 불친절한
safe 안전한

1 Anna is full.

→ _____

2 Mr. Baker is rich.

→ _____

3 My teacher is young.

→ _____

4 The lake is clean.

→ _____

5 It's cold today.

→ _____

6 The house is big.

→ _____

7 The furniture is heavy.

→ _____

8 It is dark here.

→ _____

9 The nurse is kind.

→ _____

10 This street is dangerous.

→ _____

다음 괄호 안의 단어를 참고하여 우리말과 같도록 문장을 완성하세요.

heavy 무거운
thin 마른
swimming suit
수영복

1 이 가방들은 무겁다. (bags, heavy)

→ _____

2 저 작은 소년은 영리하다. (boy, little)

→ _____

3 저 말들은 매우 빠르다. (fast, horses)

→ _____

4 그 물은 차갑지 않다. (cold, water)

→ _____

5 그녀는 부지런하고 친절하다. (diligent, kind, and)

→ _____

6 나의 아버지는 마르고 키가 크다. (thin, and, tall)

→ _____

7 내 남동생과 나는 배가 고프다. (brother, hungry)

→ _____

8 이 수영복은 젖어 있다. (wet, swimming suit)

→ _____

9 그 창문이 열려 있다. (window, open)

→ _____

10 이 그림들은 훌륭하다. (great, pictures)

→ _____

다음 빈칸에 알맞은 말을 쓰세요.

Ⅰ 형용사의 의미와 종류

• 형용사란 _____를 꾸며 주거나 설명해 주는 말로, '_____'이라는 의미이다.

• 형용사에는 지시형용사, 수량형용사, 성질형용사가 있다.

_____형용사	this, that, these, those
수량형용사	one, two, three, many, much, a lot of ...
_____형용사	상태, 색깔, 날씨, 맛 등을 나타내는 형용사 beautiful, red, cold, sweet

2 형용사의 쓰임

• 형용사는 명사 바로 앞에 와서 명사를 꾸며 주는 데, 이를 형용사의 '_____ 용법'이라고 한다.

• 형용사는 _____를 보충 설명해 주는 역할을 한다. 이때, 형용사가 _____ 뒤에 온다.

이를 형용사의 '_____ 용법'이라고 한다.

3 형용사의 위치

• 형용사의 한정적 용법에서 형용사의 위치에 유의한다.

① 형용사만 있는 경우, '_____+_____' 순서로 온다.

② 부사가 함께 오는 경우, 'a/an+_____+_____+명사' 순서로 온다.

③ 소유격이 함께 오는 경우, '_____+형용사+명사' 순서로 온다.

④ 형용사가 2개 이상일 경우, '지시형용사+_____형용사+_____형용사+명사' 순서로 온다.

Jump Up 2

다음 두 문장이 같도록 〈형용사+명사〉 형태로 고쳐 쓰세요.

interesting 재미있는
bottle 병
watch 손목시계

1   This dress is long.
   → This is a _____

2   The girls are very pretty.
   → They are very _____

3   These books are very interesting.
   → _____

4   This bottle is very clean.
   → _____

5   That park is beautiful.
   → _____

6   This singer is famous.
   → _____

7   This jacket is very small.
   → _____

8   This sweater is yellow.
   → _____

9   This watch is very expensive.
   → _____

10 Those elephants are very big.
   → _____

형용사 · **87**

다음 문장에서 틀린 부분을 바르게 고쳐 문장을 다시 쓰세요.

roof 지붕
excellent 훌륭한
cook 요리사

1   She is busy a girl.

→ _____

2   Those balls aren't bigs.

→ _____

3   That is very a hungry bear.

→ _____

4   They smart are students.

→ _____

5   These roofs are a green.

→ _____

6   I live in old this big house.

→ _____

7   Jack is very an excellent cook.

→ _____

8   My father very is angry.

→ _____

9   Jim and Olivia are very actors famous.

→ _____

10   Those are new five televisions.

→ _____

다음 주어진 두 문장을 한 문장으로 고쳐 쓰세요.

player 운동선수
hat 모자
place 장소
cookie 쿠키

1   He is a player. He is very busy.
→ He is a _____

2   She has a dog. It is very pretty.
→ _____

3   That is his car. It is white.
→ _____

4   Jake is a teacher. He is very kind.
→ _____

5   That is a house. It is expensive.
→ _____

6   It is water. It is very hot.
→ _____

7   This is a dictionary. It is very new.
→ _____

8   They are their hats. They are pink.
→ _____

9   Those are places. They are very beautiful.
→ _____

10 Those are cookies. They are sweet.
→ _____

[1~2] 다음 중 반대말끼리 짝지어지지 <u>않은</u> 것을 고르세요.

1
① old – young
② slow – fast
③ young – old
④ easy – clean

2
① low – high
② tall – short
③ hot – warm
④ heavy – light

[3~4] 다음 괄호 안의 단어가 순서에 맞게 배열된 것을 고르세요.

3 Chess is (interesting, an, game, very).
① very an interesting game
② an interesting game very
③ a very interesting game
④ very interesting a game

4 He has (expensive, and, a, old, watch).
① an old watch and expensive
② an expensive and old watch
③ an watch expensive and old
④ expensive and old a watch

[5~6] 다음 문장을 복수형으로 바르게 바꾸어 쓴 것을 고르세요.

5 That house is big.
① That houses are big.
② Those house are big.
③ Those houses is big.
④ Those houses are big.

6 This wet umbrella is mine.
① This wet umbrellas is mine.
② These wet umbrellas are mine.
③ These wet umbrella is mine.
④ These wet umbrellas is mine.

[7~8] 다음 중 올바른 문장을 고르세요.

7
① Ms. Lee is my a kind teacher.
② These are yellow three flowers.
③ You are very a smart girl.
④ That is his red car.

8
① This is a heavy bag.
② Dogs are good our friends.
③ Those are high very buildings.
④ The man is very a small and thin farmer.

9 다음 우리말과 같도록 문장을 쓰세요.

나의 빨간색 상자는 무겁다.

→ _____

[10~11] 다음 괄호 안의 단어를 바르게 배열하여 문장을 쓰세요.

10

나의 아버지는 매우 용감하고 친절한 경찰관이시다.
(brave, police officer, very, and, my, father, a, kind, is)

→ _____

11

저 많은 흰 꽃들은 공원에 있다.
(These, the park, are, in, white, flowers, many,)

→ _____

[12~13] 다음 중 짝지어진 단어의 관계가 나머지와 다른 것을 고르세요.

12 ① kind – unkind   ② cloud – cloudy
③ salt – salty   ④ love – lovely

13 ① wind – windy
② rain – rainy
③ friend – friendly
④ happy – happily

[14~16] 다음 중 밑줄 친 형용사의 쓰임이 다른 것을 고르세요.

14 ① This is a long river.
② It is my new computer.
③ The book is very interesting.
④ I borrow his blue jacket.

15 ① I love her great paintings.
② The market is open.
③ This man is very rich.
④ Those four girls are pretty.

16 ① They are kind women.
② We eat fresh apples.
③ I have a blue skirt.
④ The building is famous.

[17~18] 다음 문장의 의미와 같도록 빈칸에 알맞은 형용사를 쓰세요.

17 John is tall and thin.
= John isn't _____ and _____.

18 The city is safe and clean.
= The city isn't _____ and _____.

[19~20] 다음 문장에서 틀린 곳을 바르게 고쳐 다시 쓰세요.

19 These computers very are expensive.
→ _____

20 He is very a wise boy.
→ _____

서술형 평가

A 다음 한 문장을 두 문장으로 바꿔 쓸 때, 빈칸에 알맞은 말을 쓰세요.

1 She is a careful driver.

= She is a _____. She _____ _____.

2 We watch a interesting movie.

= We watch a _____. It _____ _____.

B 다음 그림을 묘사하는 글을 완성하세요.

There is a big house. The roof is _____. The _____ man and the
　　　　　　　　　　　　　　　　　초록색의　　　　　　　　키가 큰
boy clean the car. There are many _____ flowers in the yard.
　　　　　　　　　　　　　　　　　　　빨간색의
The woman has a cute kitty. The kitty is _____ and small. The girl plays
　　　　　　　　　　　　　　　　　　　　　　검정색의
with a _____ dog.
　　　　　　큰

Some, Any, All, Every

some과 any의 뜻과 쓰임을 이해하고 활용할 수 있다.

all의 뜻과 쓰임을 이해하고 활용할 수 있다.

every의 뜻과 쓰임을 이해하고 활용할 수 있다.

some과 any는 '몇몇의, 약간의'라는 뜻으로 많지 않은 수를 나타내요. some은 긍정

문과 권유에 사용하고 any는 의문문과 부정문에서 사용해요.

every와 all은 '모든 ~'의 뜻을 가져요.

Unit 5

Some, Any, All, Every

1. Some & any

some과 any는 '몇몇의, 약간의'라는 뜻으로 많지 않은 수를 나타낸다. some은 긍정문, 권유 및 요청에 사용하고 any는 의문문, 부정문에서 사용한다.

some	긍정문	I have some pencils. 나는 몇 개의 연필을 가지고 있다.
	권유, 제안	Would you like some milk? 우유 좀 마실래? Do you want some food? 음식 좀 드시겠어요?
	요청	Can I have some water? 물 좀 마실 수 있을까요?
any	부정문	I don't have any pencils. 나는 약간의 연필도 가지고 있지 않다.
	의문문	Do you have any pencils? 너는 약간의 연필을 가지고 있니?

• some이나 any 뒤에는 셀 수 있는 명사와 셀 수 없는 명사 모두 올 수 있다.

　단, 셀 수 있는 명사는 반드시 복수 형태로 쓴다.

　I have some toys. (O) 나는 약간의 장난감을 가지고 있다.

　I have some toy. (×)

　You don't have any stamps. (O) 너는 약간의 우표도 가지고 있지 않다.

　You don't have any stamp. (×)

• 셀 수 없는 명사는 복수 형태로 쓸 수 없다.

　I drink some coffee. (O) 나는 약간의 커피를 마신다.

　I drink some coffees. (×)

　She doesn't have any food. (O) 그녀는 약간의 음식을 먹지 않는다.

　She doesn't have any foods. (×)

Pop Quiz

1. 다음 괄호 안에서 알맞은 것을 고르세요.
   ❶ Would you like (some, any) juice?
   ❷ I don't have (some, any) money.

2. every & all

every와 all은 '모든 ~'의 뜻을 가진다.

every	every + 단수명사	every 다음에는 반드시 단수명사가 오며, 단수로 취급한다. every day 매일
	주어로 오는 경우 수 일치	「every+단수명사」 뒤에 be동사가 올 경우, 단수 형태인 is가 온다 Every student is late. 모든 학생이 늦었다.
		「every+단수명사」 뒤에 일반동사가 오는 경우, 3인칭 단수 현재형으로 온다. Every cat likes milk. 모든 고양이가 우유를 좋아한다.
all	all + 복수명사	all 다음에는 반드시 복수명사가 오며, 복수로 취급한다. all members 모든 구성원들
	주어로 오는 경우 수 일치	「all+복수명사」 뒤에 be동사가 올 경우, 복수 형태인 are가 온다 All students are quiet. 모든 학생들이 조용하다.
		「all+복수명사」 뒤에 일반동사가 올 경우, -s나 -es가 붙지 않은 동사원형 이 온다. All students go to the playground. 모든 학생들이 운동장에 간다.

▶ all+셀 수 없는 명사가 올 경우, 단수동사와 함께 쓰인다.

All information is useful to us. 모든 정보는 우리에게 유용하다.

every day와 all day의 차이
– every day: 매일
– all day: 하루 종일

Pop Quiz

2. 다음 괄호 안에서 알맞은 것을 고르세요.
   ❶ All (boy, boys) are hungry.   ❷ Every (boy, boys) likes soccer.

다음 괄호 안에서 알맞은 말을 골라 동그라미 하세요.

money 돈
sound 소리
question 질문
comic book 만화책

1 They have (some, any) food.

2 Do you have (some, any) money?

3 Do you want (some, any) cookies?

4 He doesn't have (some, any) erasers.

5 He doesn't plant (some, any) trees in the garden.

6 I don't eat (some, any) food.

7 Does he watch (some, any) movies?

8 I don't hear (some, any) sounds there.

9 He makes (some, any) cake.

10 Does Cathy carry (some, any) toy boxes?

11 She buys (some, any) bread.

12 The girl asks (some, any) questions.

13 She doesn't catch (some, any) fish.

14 We buy (some, any) caps in the store.

15 They don't have (some, any) comic books.

16 Can I have (some, any) milk?

다음 괄호 안에서 알맞은 말을 골라 동그라미 하세요.

fork 포크	
information 정보	
apple pie 사과파이	
classical music 클래식 음악	

1 I have (some, any) dishes.

2 They don't have any (carrot, carrots).

3 She has some (ball, balls).

4 They don't buy (some, any) flowers.

5 Do you need (some, any) forks?

6 Can you get any (food, foods)?

7 He can't get any (information, informations).

8 Bill doesn't have any (pet, pets).

9 Does he sell (some, any) tickets?

10 Do you want (some, any) apple pies?

11 He needs some (sugar, sugars).

12 My grandmother makes some (dress, dresses).

13 Do you listen to (some, any) classical music?

14 She reads (some, any) interesting books.

15 He sends (some, any) letters.

16 He doesn't have (some, any) laptops.

다음 괄호 안에서 알맞은 말을 골라 동그라미 하세요.

1   We play baseball (every, all) Saturday.

2   (Every, All) students arrive on time.

3   (Every, All) the flowers are red.

4   We meet him (every, all) day.

5   We watch (every, all) TV dramas.

6   The store closes (every, all) holiday.

7   I visit my grandparents (every, all) week.

8   (Every, All) morning my mom wakes me up.

9   (Every, All) boys always chat during the break.

10   (Every, All) one, attention please!

11   (Every, All) men cross the street.

12   I travel abroad (every, all) summer vacation.

13   (Every, All) doctors are in the room.

14   I wash my face (every, all) morning.

15   (Every, All) winter we go skiing.

16   She goes to the beach (every, all) summer.

on time 제 시간에
holiday 휴일
chat 수다를 떨다
during ~ 동안
break 쉬는 시간
attention 집중하다
beach 해변

Check Up 4

다음 괄호 안에서 알맞은 말을 골라 동그라미 하세요.

1 Every person (needs, need) love.

2 All children (likes, like) ice-cream.

3 Every book (are, is) on the table.

4 All trees (is, are) tall.

5 Every child (want, wants) to play with toys.

6 All Koreans (eats, eat) kimchi.

7 All boys (are, is) good at playing games.

8 Every student (passes, pass) the test.

9 All girls (play, plays) tennis after school.

10 Every man (has, have) future plans.

11 All parents (love, loves) their children.

12 All sports (is, are) good for our health.

13 Every boy (want, wants) true friends.

14 All monkeys (like, likes) bananas.

15 All doctors (is, are) busy now.

16 Every (policeman, policemen) helps them.

person 사람
pass 통과하다
future 미래, 장래
health 건강
true 진정한

다음 문장의 빈칸에 some이나 any 중에서 알맞을 것을 쓰세요.

classmate 급우
strawberry 딸기

1 We don't have _____ money.

2 Do you collect _____ stamps?

3 He meets _____ classmates.

4 You don't watch _____ TV shows.

5 Does Sue sell _____ bags?

6 She doesn't give _____ information to him.

7 We plant _____ trees in the mountain.

8 They don't wash _____ strawberries.

9 Does she drink _____ water?

10 Would you like _____ tea?

11 We don't carry _____ boxes.

12 Does she ask _____ questions about it?

13 We see _____ elephants in the zoo.

14 He doesn't buy _____ sneakers.

15 Could you pass me _____ salt?

16 Can I have _____ soup?

다음 문장의 빈칸에 every와 all 중에서 알맞을 것을 쓰세요.

picnic 소풍
quiet 조용한
eat out 외식하다

1　We go to the beach _____ summer.

2　I drink juice _____ day.

3　_____ students are good at computer.

4　_____ children sleep well for their health.

5　_____ spring, they go on a picnic.

6　_____ her friends are very smart.

7　_____ giraffes are very quiet.

8　_____ the students go to the summer camp.

9　_____ policeman helps us.

10　_____ mother loves her children.

11　My family eats out _____ Saturday evening.

12　He doesn't work _____ weekend.

13　In this town, _____ kid speaks Korean.

14　She doesn't send _____ letters to him.

15　I like _____ my team members.

16　_____ Friday, I watch a movie with my friends.

다음 괄호 안의 단어를 알맞은 위치에 넣어 문장을 다시 쓰세요.

fresh 신선한

cut 자르다

1 Would you like coffee? (some)

→ _____

2 They don't have fresh milk. (any)

→ _____

3 She sells beautiful red roses. (some)

→ _____

4 Does she cut tall trees? (any)

→ _____

5 His daughters want cute cats. (some)

→ _____

6 I don't eat hot soup. (any)

→ _____

7 We carry heavy boxes. (some)

→ _____

8 Do you have red T-shirts? (any)

→ _____

9 We don't have long coats. (any)

→ _____

10 Brown leaves is falling. (some)

→ _____

Build Up 2

다음 문장을 의문문과 부정문으로 바꾸어 쓰세요.

raise 기르다
poem 시

1 Joe raises some pets.

(의문문) _____

(부정문) _____

2 Your friend eats some cookies.

(의문문) _____

(부정문) _____

3 He writes some poems.

(의문문) _____

(부정문) _____

4 Her father helps some poor people.

(의문문) _____

(부정문) _____

5 They visit some kids everyday.

(의문문) _____

(부정문) _____

6 He sells some vegetables.

(의문문) _____

(부정문) _____

7 She teaches some young students.

(의문문) _____

(부정문) _____

다음 우리말과 같도록 문장을 완성하세요.

outside 바깥
e-mail 이메일

1 doesn't / student / go / every / to school
모든 학생들이 학교에 가지 않는다.
→ _____

2 have / do / any / friends / you
너는 몇몇의 친구가 있니?
→ _____

3 children / all / play / outside
모든 아이들이 바깥에서 논다.
→ _____

4 you / like / would / orange juice / some
오렌지주스 좀 마시겠습니까?
→ _____

5 Friday / play / we / soccer / every
우리는 금요일마다 축구를 한다.
→ _____

6 e-mails / to / some / mom / send / we
우리는 엄마에게 몇 통의 이메일을 보냅니다.
→ _____

7 the handsome singer / all / girls / like
모든 소녀들이 그 잘생긴 가수를 좋아한다.
→ _____

8 I / visit / my / winter / every / vacation / uncle
매 겨울 방학 마다 나는 삼촌을 방문한다.
→ _____

다음 빈칸에 알맞은 말을 쓰세요.

Ⅰ some & any

- some과 any는 '_____, 약간의'라는 뜻으로 많지 않은 수를 나타낸다.
- some은 _____, 권유 및 요청에 사용하고 any는 _____, 부정문에서 사용한다.
- some이나 any 뒤에는 _____ 명사와 _____ 명사 모두 올 수 있다. 단, 셀 수 있는 명사는 반드시 _____ 형태로 쓴다.

	긍정문	I have _____ pencils.
_____	권유, 제안	Would you like _____ milk? Do you want _____ food? – Yes, I do.
	_____	Can I have some water?
_____	부정문	I don't have _____ pencils.
	_____	Do you have _____ pencils?

2 every & all

- every와 all은 '_____ ~'의 뜻을 가진다.
- every 다음에는 반드시 _____ 명사가 오며, 단수로 취급한다.
- 「every+단수명사」 뒤에 일반동사가 오는 경우, _____인칭 _____ 현재형으로 온다.
  「every+단수명사」 뒤에 be동사가 올 경우, 단수 형태인 _____가 온다.
- all 다음에는 반드시 _____ 명사가 오며, 복수로 취급한다.
- 「all+복수명사」 뒤에 일반동사가 올 경우, -s나 -es가 붙지 않은 동사원형이 온다.
- 「all+복수명사」 뒤에 be동사가 올 경우, 복수 형태인 _____가 온다.

다음 문장에서 틀린 부분에 밑줄을 치고 바르게 고치세요.

close 가까운, 친한
borrow 빌리다
surprising 놀라운
pour 붓다
word 단어, 말

1 I have some close friend. → _____

2 Do you sell some toys? → _____

3 Does she meet some movie stars? → _____

4 My uncle has any famous paintings. → _____

5 Does Suji borrow some books? → _____

6 Can I have any pepper for my soup? → _____

7 We have any surprising news. → _____

8 Do you have some questions? → _____

9 She wants some coffees. → _____

10 Do you build some tents? → _____

11 Some tree are very tall. → _____

12 He don't buy some books there. → _____

13 Would you drink any apple juice? → _____

14 They make any cookies. → _____

15 He pours some flours in the bowl. → _____

16 He doesn't say any word. → _____

다음 문장에서 틀린 부분에 밑줄을 치고 바르게 고치세요.

1 Do you go to the library all day? → _____

2 I fix every the clocks with my mom. → _____

3 All problem is so difficult. → _____

4 Do every snakes have poison? → _____

5 All door is locked and closed. → _____

6 Every children are smart. → _____

7 All one is glad to hear the news. → _____

8 We go on a picnic all weekend. → _____

9 Every boys are good at playing games. → _____

10 He gives every flowers to her. → _____

11 Our team wins every the games. → _____

12 We go to the market all weekend. → _____

13 They send postcards to him all week. → _____

14 She searches all information about the accident.

    → _____

15 He brings us every the umbrellas. → _____

16 We go to school all morning. → _____

fix 고치다, 수리하다
poison 독
locked 잠긴
search 찾다
accident 사건

다음 괄호 안의 단어를 참고하여 우리말과 같도록 문장을 완성하세요.

arrive 도착하다
wait for 기다리다
come true 실현되다

1 나는 몇몇 친구들을 본다. (see, some)

→ I _____

2 너는 매주 일요일에 교회에 가니? (every, church)

→ Do you _____

3 이 빵 좀 먹을래? (want, some)

→ Do you _____

4 나는 어떤 질문도 없다. (any, have)

→ I don't _____

5 모든 학생들이 제시간에 도착한다. (arrive, all)

→ _____ on time.

6 음식 좀 먹을 수 있을까? (some, have)

→ Can I _____

7 나는 어떤 정보도 찾을 수 없다. (any, information, find)

→ I can't _____

8 모든 사람이 그를 기다린다. (wait for, every, one)

→ _____

9 모든 희망이 이루어진다. (every, come true, hope)

→ _____

10 모든 아이들이 그 선생님을 좋아한다. (all, like, children)

→ _____

[1~2] 다음 중 빈칸에 들어갈 말로 알맞지 <u>않은</u> 것을 고르세요.

1 I have some _____.
① books   ② pencils
③ sugars   ④ knives

2 Every _____ likes cats.
① children   ② girl
③ boy   ④ woman

[3~4] 다음 중 빈칸에 들어갈 말이 <u>다른</u> 것을 고르세요.

3 ① He eats _____ pizza.
② She buys _____ comic books.
③ We don't have _____ money.
④ I want _____ holidays.

4 ① _____ the windows are open.
② I love _____ my children.
③ _____ boys are on the playground.
④ He visit his grandmother _____ Sunday.

5 다음 문장을 부정문으로 바르게 바꾸어 쓴 것을 고르세요.

> She has some interesting books about birds.

① She don't has some interesting books about birds.
② She don't have any interesting books about birds.
③ She doesn't have some interesting books about birds.
④ She doesn't have any interesting books about birds.

6 다음 문장을 의문문으로 바르게 바꾸어 쓴 것을 고르세요.

> He buys some food for dinner.

① Do he buys some food for dinner?
② Does he buy any food for dinner?
③ Does he buys any food for dinner?
④ Does he buy some food for dinner?

[7~8] 다음 빈칸에 some과 any 중에서 알맞은 말을 쓰세요.

7
> A: Would you like _____ apple pies?
> B: Yes, please.

→ _____

8

> I don't have _____ brothers and sisters.

→ _____

[9~10] 다음 빈칸에 들어갈 말로 알맞은 것을 고르세요.

9 All girls _____ the puppy.

① likes　　② hates

③ love　　④ wishes

10 Every city _____ clean in the country.

① be　　② is

③ am　　④ are

[11~12] 다음 주어진 단어를 이용해 문장을 쓰세요.

11 이 케이크 좀 먹을래?

(some, cake, want)

→ _____

12 모든 학생들이 제시간에 도착한다.

(on time, all, arrive)

→ _____

[13~14] 다음 문장에서 틀린 곳을 바르게 고쳐 다시 쓰세요.

13 Do you have some questions?

→ _____

14 All information are useful to him.

→ _____

[15~18] 다음 빈칸에 들어갈 말이 순서대로 짝 지어진 것을 고르세요.

15

> · Can I have _____ hot milk?
> · Do you build _____ houses?

① any – any

② any – some

③ some – any

④ some – some

16

> · There aren't _____ students in the gym.
> · Jane buys _____ balloons for the party.

① any – any

② any – some

③ some – any

④ some – some

17

> · _____ children like computer games.
> · She meets her best friend _____ Saturday.

① all – all

② all – every

③ every – all

④ every – every

18

> · I love _____ animals.
> · _____ dogs are faithful.
> · _____ cat is smart.

① all – all – all

② every – all – all

③ all – all – every

④ every – all – every

[19~20] 괄호 안의 단어를 바르게 배열하여 문장을 쓰세요.

19

> 우리 가족은 주말마다 캠핑을 간다.
> (my family, every, camping, weekend, goes)

→ _____

20

> 모든 뱀이 독을 가지고 있습니까?
> (snakes, poison, all, have, do, ?)

→ _____

A 다음 그림을 묘사하는 글을 some, any, all, every를 써서 완성하세요.

1 _____ students are in the classroom.

2 The students don't eat _____ cookies.

3 _____ boy looks out of the windows.

4 _____ girls listen to music.

B 옷가게 안에서 점원과 손님의 대화를 완성하세요.

A: Do you have _____ white T-shirts?

B: Yes, we have _____ white T-shirts.
How about this one?

A: Do you have _____ V necks?

B: Umm. Sorry.

_____ white T-shirt is round neck.

Unit 6

수량형용사

수량형용사의 종류와 쓰임을 이해하고 활용할 수 있다.

수량형용사와 수의 일치를 이해하고 활용할 수 있다.

many, a few, few는 셀 수 있는 명사 앞에 쓰며, much, a little, little은 셀 수 없는 명사 앞에 쓰여요. a lot of는 셀 수 있는 명사와 셀 수 없는 명사의 앞에 모두 쓰여요.

Unit 6

수량형용사

1. many, much, a lot of(lots of)

'많이'나 '조금'과 같이 수량을 나타내는 형용사를 수량형용사라고 하는데 many, much, a lot of(lots of)는 '많은'이라는 의미이다.

- many는 셀 수 있는 명사 앞에 쓰여서 수가 많음을 나타낸다.

  many children 많은 아이들   many balls 많은 공들

  many books 많은 책들   many computers 많은 컴퓨터들

- much는 셀 수 없는 명사 앞에 쓰여서 양이 많음을 나타낸다.

  much time 많은 시간   much love 많은 사랑

  much money 많은 돈   much soup 많은 수프

- a lot of는 셀 수 있는 명사와 셀 수 없는 명사 앞에 모두 쓸 수 있다.

  a lot of books 많은 책들   a lot of children 많은 아이들

  a lot of time 많은 시간   a lot of soup 많은 수프

- many와 a lot of는 긍정문, 의문문, 부정문 모두에 사용된다. much는 보통 의문문, 부정문에만 사용되고, 긍정문에는 주로 a lot of를 사용한다.

  〈many, a lot of〉

  긍정문   I have many friends. 나는 많은 친구들을 가지고 있다.

  = I have a lot of friends.

  의문문   Do you have many friends? 너는 많은 친구들을 가지고 있니?

  = Do you have a lot of friends?

부정문   You don't have many friends. 너는 많은 친구들이 없다.
          = You don't have a lot of friends.

〈much, a lot of〉

긍정문   I eat much soup. (×)
          = I eat a lot of soup. (○) 나는 많은 수프를 먹는다.

의문문   Do you eat much soup? 너는 많은 수프를 먹니?
          = Do you eat a lot of soup?

부정문   You don't eat much soup. 너는 많은 수프를 먹지 않는다.
          = You don't eat a lot of soup.

Pop Quiz   1. 다음 괄호 안에서 알맞은 말에 동그라미하세요.
            ❶ Do you have (many, much) books?
            ❷ He doesn't drink (many, much) water.

2. a few, a little, few, little

a few와 a little은 '약간의', '조금의'라는 의미이고, few와 little은 '거의 없는'이라는 의미이다.

• a few와 few는 셀 수 있는 명사 앞에 쓰이고, a little과 little은 셀 수 없는 명사 앞에 쓰인다.

수량형용사		의미	쓰임
a few (= some)	+셀 수 있는 명사 (복수형)	조금 있는, 몇몇의	a few books 몇 권의 책들
few		거의 없는	few books 책이 거의 없는
a little (= some)	+셀 수 없는 명사 (단수형)	조금 있는, 약간의	a little water 약간의 물
little		거의 없는	little water 물이 거의 없는

- a few와 a little은 긍정의 의미로 쓰이고, few와 little은 not 없이 부정의 의미를 나타낸다.

I have a few questions. 나는 약간의 질문이 있다.

I have few questions. 나는 질문이 거의 없다.

I drink a little milk. 나는 약간의 우유를 마신다.

I drink little milk. 나는 우유를 거의 마시지 않는다.

3. 수량형용사의 수 일치

- many, a few, few는 셀 수 있는 명사의 복수형 앞에서 쓰이고, much, a little, little은 셀 수 없는 명사 앞에서 쓰인다.

- a lot of, lots of, some, any는 셀 수 있는 명사의 복수형과 셀 수 없는 명사 앞에 모두 쓰인다.

many, a few, few	+셀 수 있는 명사(복수형)
much, a little, little	+셀 수 없는 명사
a lot of, lots of, some, any	+셀 수 있는 명사(복수형)
	+셀 수 없는 명사

Pop Quiz   2. 다음 괄호 안에서 알맞은 것을 고르세요.
❶ She eats (a few, a little) meat.
❷ I have (few, little) toys.

다음 괄호 안에서 알맞은 말을 골라 동그라미 하세요.

1 She has (many, much) pencils.

2 He doesn't drink (many, much) coffee.

3 (Many, Much) policemen don't go to the city.

4 (Many, Much) people are on the street.

5 Do they eat (many, much) pizza?

6 The writer travels (many, much) countries.

7 We don't eat (many, much) salt.

8 We have (many, much) classes on Tuesday.

9 (Many, Much) deer are in the forest.

10 He counts (many, much) coins.

11 Do you take (many, much) good photos?

12 The girl doesn't eat (many, much) cake.

13 David doesn't sell (many, much) fruits.

14 (Many, Much) bees are in the hive.

15 (Many, Much) cheese isn't in the store.

16 Mary wears (many, much) accessories.

travel 여행하다
forest 숲
hive 벌집
wear 입다, 걸치다
accessory 액세서리

다음 괄호 안에서 알맞은 말을 골라 동그라미 하세요.

spend 소비하다
washing machine
세탁기
desert 사막
pain 통증
snack 간식

1   There is (much, a lot of) jam in the jar.

2   He doesn't have (much, many) ice cream.

3   He drinks (a lot of, many) milk.

4   They buy (much, a lot of) apples.

5   My son eats (much, many) cookies.

6   Julie doesn't have (much, many) time for the test.

7   Do they make (much, many) soup?

8   The washing machine needs (a lot of, many) water.

9   She finds (much, a lot of) oil in the desert.

10   Is there (much, many) snow in Canada?

11   Amy doesn't drink (many, much) juice.

12   The driver feels (many, a lot of) pain.

13   Olivia buys (many, a lot of) meat.

14   Do you eat (much, many) snack?

15   She spends (many, a lot of) money for shopping.

16   He has (many, a lot of) food for dinner.

다음 괄호 안에서 알맞은 말을 골라 동그라미 하세요.

meal 식사
space 공간
writer 작가

1   He has (a little, a few) classes on Friday.

2   The kid eats (a little, a few) rice every meal.

3   Do you use (a little, a few) dishes?

4   The laptops need (a little, a few) space.

5   My mother puts (little, few) salt in the food.

6   We have (a little, a few) rain in spring.

7   She takes (little, few) photos there.

8   We buy (little, few) flour in the store.

9   He looks at (a little, a few) stars in the sky.

10   He draws (little, few) people.

11   The children see (little, few) animals in the zoo.

12   I eat (little, few) meat for lunch.

13   I speak (a little, a few) English.

14   Peter fixes (little, few) computers.

15   He does (a little, a few) work on Monday.

16   The writer visits (little, few) foreign countries.

다음 괄호 안에서 알맞은 말을 골라 동그라미 하세요.

cloth 옷, 의류
bread 빵
idea 생각, 아이디어
shampoo 샴푸

1 She has a few (toy, toys).

2 We buy a few (flower, flowers).

3 We have a little (snow, snows) in winter.

4 He does little (work, works) every day.

5 The car needs a little (oil, oils).

6 I have a few (chair, chairs) here.

7 She spends little (money, moneys).

8 Do you have a few (cloth, clothes)?

9 We use little (shampoo, shampoos).

10 Her son reads few (comic book, comic books).

11 My brother eats little (bread, breads).

12 I have a few (idea, ideas).

13 I know few (name, names) in the office.

14 I have little (tea, teas) for the meeting.

15 He drinks little (water, waters) in summer.

16 He makes a few (cookie, cookies) for her.

다음 빈칸에 알맞은 말을 〈보기〉에서 골라 쓰세요.

| sick 아픈 |
| paper cup 종이컵 |
| carrot 당근 |
| help 도움 |

〈보기〉   a few   few   a little   little

1 The doctor cures _____ sick people.

의사는 몇몇 아픈 사람들을 치료한다.

2 He eats _____ sugar.

그는 설탕을 조금 먹는다.

3 _____ glasses are on the table.

탁자 위에 몇 개의 유리컵이 있다.

4 _____ cheese is in the bowl.

치즈가 그릇 안에 거의 없다.

5 I use _____ paper cups.

나는 종이컵을 거의 사용하지 않는다.

6 Do you have _____ cake?

케이크가 조금 있습니까?

7 She has _____ information about him.

그녀는 그에 대한 정보가 거의 없다.

8 The rabbit eats _____ carrots.

토끼는 약간의 당근을 먹는다.

9 The boy needs _____ help.

소년은 도움이 거의 필요 없다.

10 He has _____ money in his pocket.

그는 주머니에 약간의 돈이 있다.

다음 빈칸에 알맞은 말을 〈보기〉에서 골라 쓰세요.

different 다른
language 언어
bake 굽다

〈보기〉 a little little many much a few few

1 The women need _____ milk.

그 여자들은 약간의 우유가 필요하다.

2 Do you have _____ books in your bag?

가방에 책이 몇 권 있니?

3 I play soccer with _____ kids.

나는 많은 아이들과 축구를 한다.

4 Lisa doesn't drink _____ coffee in the evening.

Lisa는 저녁에 많은 커피를 마시지 않는다.

5 She speaks _____ different languages.

그녀는 몇 개의 다른 언어를 말한다.

6 My mom doesn't bake _____ bread.

우리 엄마는 많은 빵을 굽지 않는다.

7 _____ people are in the museum.

많은 사람들이 박물관에 있다.

8 The children eat _____ hamburgers.

그 어린이들은 햄버거를 거의 먹지 않는다.

9 _____ hotels are closed on the holidays.

몇 개의 호텔들이 휴일에는 문을 닫는다.

10 The teacher gives _____ homework to students.

그 선생님은 학생들에게 숙제를 거의 내주지 않는다.

다음 빈칸에 many, much, a lot of를 쓰세요. (2가지 가능하면 2가지 모두 쓸 것)

hurry 서두르다
mistake 실수
gas 가스
luck 행운, 운

1 The boy drinks _____ water.

2 I have _____ friends in school.

3 We have _____ fruits in the refrigerator.

4 Hurry up! We don't have _____ time.

5 We have _____ food at home.

6 He doesn't drink _____ tea.

7 We have _____ beautiful cups.

8 The boys see _____ buildings in this town.

9 We don't have _____ money in our pocket.

10 Judy speaks _____ different languages.

11 We have _____ rain in summer.

12 I made _____ mistakes.

13 _____ students pass the exam.

14 I don't have _____ gas.

15 I need _____ luck.

다음 빈칸에 a few, few, a little, little 중 알맞은 것을 쓰세요.

oxygen 산소
tank 탱크, 통
honey 꿀
yogurt 요구르트
air 공기

1 There is _____ oxygen in the tank.
   저 탱크 안에는 산소가 거의 없다.

2 He has _____ friends in his school.
   그는 학교에 몇몇의 친구가 있다.

3 We have _____ snow in February.
   눈이 2월에는 거의 오지 않는다.

4 There are _____ museums in the city.
   그 도시에는 박물관이 거의 없다.

5 The cook uses _____ honey.
   요리사는 약간의 꿀을 사용한다.

6 He needs _____ onions.
   그는 몇 개의 양파가 필요하다.

7 The kid eat _____ yogurt every morning.
   아이는 매일 아침 약간의 요구르트를 먹는다.

8 _____ ships are in the sea.
   몇 개의 배가 바다에 있다.

9 _____ air is in the tube.
   튜브에는 공기가 거의 없다.

10 She has _____ summer clothes.
   그녀는 여름옷이 거의 없다.

다음 괄호 안의 말과 수량형용사를 사용하여 문장을 완성하세요.

chocolate 초콜릿
mailbox 우편함

1 _____ is in this box. (chocolate)

이 상자 안에 초콜릿이 약간 있다.

2 There are _____ in Korea. (mountain)

한국에는 많은 산들이 있다.

3 I have _____ today. (homework)

오늘 나는 숙제가 거의 없다.

4 I pour _____ into the bowl. (flour)

나는 약간의 밀가루를 그릇에 붓는다.

5 He doesn't buy _____. (food)

그는 많은 음식을 사지 않는다.

6 She makes _____ for her niece. (doll)

그녀는 그녀의 조카에게 줄 인형을 몇 개 만든다.

7 _____ are in the mailbox. (letter)

우편함에 거의 편지가 없다.

8 My sister eats _____. (cheese)

나의 언니는 치즈를 거의 먹지 않는다.

9 _____ are in this town. (restaurant)

수많은 식당들이 이 마을에 있다.

10 She doesn't get _____. (information)

그녀는 많은 정보를 얻지 못한다.

다음 빈칸에 알맞은 말을 쓰세요.

1 many, much, a lot of[lots of]

- '_____' 이라는 의미이다.
- many는 _____ 명사 앞에 쓰여서 수가 많음을 나타낸다.
- much는 _____ 명사 앞에 쓰여서 양이 많음을 나타낸다.
- _____[lots of]는 셀 수 있는 명사와 셀 수 없는 명사 앞에 모두 쓸 수 있다.
- many와 a lot of는 긍정문, 의문문, 부정문 모두에 사용하고, much는 _____, _____ 에만 사용한다.

2 a few, few, a little, little

- a few와 a little은 '_____', '조금의'라는 의미이고, few와 little은 '_____'이 라는 의미이다.
- a few와 few는 _____ 명사 앞에 쓰이고, a little과 little은 _____ 명사 앞에 쓰인다.
- _____와 a little은 긍정의 의미로 쓰이고, few와 _____은 not 없이 부정의 의미 를 나타낸다.

3 수량형용사의 수 일치

- many, _____, few는 셀 수 있는 명사의 _____ 앞에 쓰고, _____, a little, _____은 셀 수 없는 명사 앞에 쓴다.
- a lot of, lots of, some, any는 셀 수 있는 명사의 _____과 셀 수 없는 명사 앞에 모두 쓰인다.

다음 문장의 밑줄 친 부분을 바르게 고쳐 쓰세요.

coke 콜라
hit 치다
pond 연못

1 We don't have <u>many</u> rain in spring. → _____

2 The girl drinks <u>few</u> coke. → _____

3 The player hits <u>much</u> balls. → _____

4 Does she eat <u>many</u> meat? → _____

5 <u>Little</u> hospitals are in this town. → _____

6 She mixes <u>many</u> flour in the bowl. → _____

7 I meet a few <u>singer</u>. → _____

8 She watches <u>little</u> soccer games. → _____

9 We read <u>much</u> comic books every year. → _____

10 <u>A little</u> students are in the gym. → _____

11 I buy <u>much</u> butter in the store. → _____

12 My mother sends <u>little</u> postcards. → _____

13 The woman uses <u>a few</u> honey. → _____

14 I drink <u>few</u> milk in the morning. → _____

15 <u>Much</u> fish are in the pond. → _____

16 He eats <u>a few</u> food for breakfast. → _____

다음 문장에서 틀린 부분에 동그라미 하고 바르게 고쳐 쓰세요.

hour 시간
pitcher 투수
catch 잡다
closet 옷장

1 We need a little ices. → _____

2 She bakes a few bread every day. → _____

3 They need a little hours. → _____

4 The pitcher catches many ball. → _____

5 Diane has much clothes in the closet. → _____

6 A few pant are small. → _____

7 We have few snow in winter. → _____

8 She watches little movies. → _____

9 We read much books every year. → _____

10 Many student study at the library. → _____

11 I have much money in the purse. → _____

12 My mother writes much poems. → _____

13 Much leaves fall down in autumn. → _____

14 A lot of sugar are in the bag. → _____

15 Many child play on the playground. → _____

16 He visits Japan many time. → _____

다음 〈보기〉의 수량형용사와 제시된 말을 사용해 문장을 완성하세요.

market 시장

〈보기〉 a little little a few few many a lot of much

1 그는 개 몇 마리가 있다. (dog)
→ He has _____ .

2 그녀는 약간의 도움이 필요하다. (need, help)
→ She _____ .

3 나의 아들은 책을 거의 읽지 않는다. (book, read)
→ My son _____ .

4 그는 겨울에는 물을 거의 마시지 않는다. (water, drink)
→ _____ in winter.

5 많은 나무들이 숲에 있다. (tree)
→ _____ are in the forest.

6 빵이 그 바구니 안에 많이 있다. (bread)
→ _____ is in the basket.

7 나는 영어를 거의 말하지 않는다. (speak, English)
→ I _____ .

8 Jake는 시장에서 많은 고기를 산다. (meat, buy)
→ _____ at the market.

9 올해는 휴일이 많다. (holiday, have)
→ _____ this year.

실전 평가

[1~3] 다음 문장의 빈칸에 들어갈 알맞은 말을 고르세요.

1 He has many _____.
① time   ② luck
③ cake   ④ friends

2 They don't need much _____.
① chairs   ② clothes
③ food   ④ books

3 She eats little _____.
① lemons   ② candies
③ meat   ④ chocolates

[4~5] 다음 문장의 밑줄 친 부분과 바꾸어 쓸 수 있는 말을 고르세요.

4 Do you buy <u>many</u> CDs?
① a little   ② a lot of
③ much   ④ little

5 She needs <u>some</u> help.
① a little   ② many
③ much   ④ a few

6 다음 중 a few와 함께 쓰일 수 <u>없는</u> 명사를 고르세요.
① apple   ② coin
③ sugar   ④ monkey

7 다음 빈칸에 공통으로 들어갈 말을 쓰세요.

> · He eats _____ cookies.
> · They get _____ information.

→ _____

[8~9] 다음 밑줄 친 부분을 바르게 고친 것을 고르세요.

8 I know <u>a little</u> teacher.
① little teacher.   ② a little teachers
③ few teacher   ④ a few teachers

9 He travels <u>much countries</u>.
① much country
② a lot of country
③ many countries
④ little countries

[10~12] 다음 중 밑줄 친 부분이 <u>잘못된</u> 문장을 고르세요.

10 ① John sells <u>a lot of</u> toys.
② Do you remember <u>many</u> names?
③ We need <u>a little</u> sugar.
④ Mary eats <u>a little</u> sandwiches.

11 ① They eat <u>a lot of</u> bread.
② The policeman has <u>few</u> guns.
③ Do you have <u>a few</u> pepper?
④ <u>Many</u> children like the song.

12 ① A lot of people like the movie.

② Does she eat many meat?

③ I drink a little tea every morning.

④ My mother makes many cookies for the party.

13 다음 중 빈칸에 들어갈 말이 바르게 짝지어 진 것을 고르세요.

> · I spend _____ time for studying.
>
> · He visits _____ countries.

① much – many

② a little – much

③ a lot of – a few

④ a few – a lot of

[14~15] 다음 문장에서 틀린 부분을 찾아 바르게 고쳐 쓰세요.

14

> My mom doesn't use much salts in her food.

_____ → _____

15

> He has a little cousins.

_____ → _____

[16~17] 다음 우리말을 영어로 올바르게 옮긴 것을 고르세요.

16 이 병에 많은 우유가 있다.

① Many milk are in this bottle.

② A lot of milk are in this bottle.

③ A lot of milk is in this bottle.

④ Much milk are in this bottle.

17 그 연못 안에 물고기가 거의 없다.

① A little fish is in the pond.

② Few fish are in the pond.

③ A few fish are in the pond.

④ Little fish is in the pond.

[18~20] 다음 우리말 뜻과 같도록 빈칸에 알맞은 말을 쓰세요.

18

> 약간의 치즈를 원하니?

Do you want _____ cheese?

19

> 그 세탁기는 물을 많이 사용하지 않는다.

The washing machine doesn't use _____ water.

20

> 나는 장난감을 사지 않는다.

I buy _____ toys.

서술형 평가

A 다음 그림을 보고, 그림을 묘사하는 문장을 완성하세요.

My mother goes shopping. She buys 1. _____ _____ _____ cheese, 2. _____

_____ tomatoes, 3. _____ _____ bread. She makes 4. _____ _____ sandwiches.

5. _____ milk is in the glass.

B 다음은 세계 각 도시의 연간 강수량을 나타낸 표입니다. 표의 내용을 보고 문장을 완성하세요.

	Seoul	New York	London	Toronto
rain	2000 mm	1000 mm	3000 mm	1000 mm
snow	15 cm	1 cm	10 cm	35 cm

1 There is _____ . 런던에는 비가 많이 온다.

2 There is _____ . 토론토에는 눈이 많이 온다.

3 There is _____ . 뉴욕에는 눈이 거의 오지 않는다.

Unit 7

부사

부사의 쓰임과 형태를 알고 활용할 수 있다.

부사를 알맞은 위치에 사용할 수 있다.

빈도부사의 종류와 쓰임을 알고 활용할 수 있다.

부사는 동사, 형용사, 다른 부사 등을 꾸며 주는 말로, 형용사 앞이나 주로 문장의 뒤에 와요. 단, 강조할 때는 문장 앞에 오기도 해요.

또한 부사 중에 빈도부사라는 것이 있는데, 빈도부사는 얼마나 자주 하는지, 횟수나 빈도를 나타내는 부사로 be동사나 조동사 뒤에, 일반동사 앞에 위치해요.

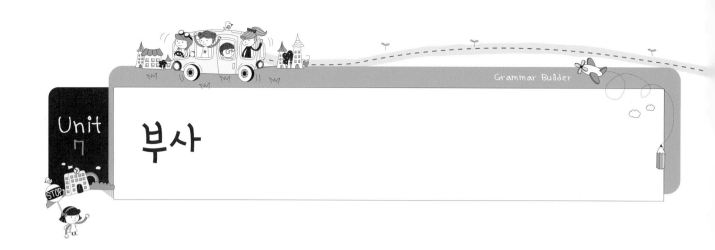

Unit
7

부사

1. 부사의 의미와 쓰임

부사란 동사, 형용사, 다른 부사 등을 꾸며 주는 말로, 보통 '~하게'라는 의미이다.

부사가 형용사를 꾸미는 경우(형용사 앞 위치)	부사가 동사를 꾸미는 경우(동사 뒤 위치)
He is a really kind doctor. 부사　형용사　명사 그는 정말 친절한 의사이다.	He comes late. 동사　부사 그는 늦게 온다.
부사가 부사를 꾸미는 경우(부사 앞 위치)	**부사가 문장 전체를 꾸미는 경우(문장 맨 앞 위치)**
He comes very late. 동사　부사　부사 그는 매우 늦게 온다.	Suddenly he falls down. 부사　　　문장 전체 갑자기 그는 넘어진다.

2. 부사의 형태

대부분의 부사는 형용사 끝에 -ly를 붙여 만든다.

bad	나쁜	+ ly →	badly	나쁘게
slow	느린	+ ly →	slowly	느리게
kind	친절한	+ ly →	kindly	친절하게
quick	빠른	+ ly →	quickly	빠르게
quiet	조용한	+ ly →	quietly	조용히
angry	화난	+ ly →	angrily	화나게

| careful | 조심스러운 | + | ly | → | carefully | 조심스럽게 |
| beautiful | 아름다운 | + | ly | → | beautifully | 아름답게 |

• 「자음+y」로 끝나는 형용사는 -y를 -i로 바꾸고 -ly를 붙인다.

busy	바쁜	+	ly	→	busily	바쁘게
easy	쉬운	+	ly	→	easily	쉽게
happy	행복한	+	ly	→	happily	행복하게
lucky	운 좋은	+	ly	→	luckily	운 좋게

> 단어에 -ly가 붙은
> 단어들이 모두 부사는 아니다.
> 명사 +-ly는 형용사가 된다.
> love 사랑 – lovely 사랑스러운

• 형용사와 부사가 같은 부사

fast 빠른 → fast 빠르게, early 이른 → early 일찍, late 늦은 → late 늦게,

high 높은 → high 높게, near 가까운 → near 가까이, hard 어려운 → hard 열심히

It is high building. 그것은 높은 건물이다. [형용사]

She can jump high. 그녀는 높이 뛸 수 있다. [부사]

• 주의해야 할 부사

-ly를 붙여 뜻이 달라지는 경우	형용사와 부사의 형태가 다른 경우
lately 최근에, highly 매우, hardly 거의 ~않은, nearly 거의	good 좋은 → well 잘

> 같은 단어가
> 형용사-부사로 쓰일 때 의미가 달라지는 경우
> → pretty 예쁜 – pretty 꽤, 매우
> well 건강한 – well 잘

Pop Quiz Ⅰ. 다음 중 부사를 찾아서 동그라미 하세요.
❶ She speaks slowly.　❷ He is a very diligent student.

3. 빈도 부사

얼마나 자주 하는지, 횟수나 빈도를 나타내는 부사를 빈도 부사라고 한다.

횟수	부사	
0%	never 결코 ~않다	I am never late. 나는 결코 늦지 않는다.
20%	rarely 거의 ~않다	I rarely put on a skirt. 나는 거의 치마를 입지 않는다.
50%	sometimes 때때로, 가끔	I sometimes play computer games. 나는 가끔 컴퓨터 게임을 한다.
60%	often 자주, 종종	I often listen to music. 나는 자주 음악을 듣는다.
80%	usually 보통	I usually have breakfast. 나는 보통 아침을 먹는다.
100%	always 항상	I always get up early. 나는 항상 일찍 일어난다.

- 빈도부사는 be동사, 조동사 뒤, 일반동사 앞에 위치한다.

He is always busy. 그는 항상 바쁘다.

He will often visit you. 그가 당신을 종종 방문할 것이다.

He comes sometimes late. 그는 가끔 늦는다.

Pop Quiz **2.** 다음 문장에서 빈도부사가 들어갈 위치를 고르세요.

❶ He ① goes ② to ③ the zoo. (sometimes)

❷ I ① will ② be ③ your friend. (always)

다음 빈칸에 알맞은 형용사나 부사를 쓰세요.

			quick 빠른

quick 빠른
easy 쉬운
well 잘

1 _____ 빠른 — **fast** 빠르게

2 **happy** 행복한 — _____ 행복하게

3 **late** 늦은 — _____ 늦게

4 **beautiful** 아름다운 — _____ 아름답게

5 _____ 나쁜 — **badly** 나쁘게

6 **slow** 느린 — _____ 느리게

7 **kind** 친절한 — _____ 친절하게

8 _____ 빠른 — **quickly** 빠르게

9 **quiet** 조용한 — _____ 조용하게

10 **careful** 조심스러운 — _____ 조심스럽게

11 _____ 쉬운 — **easily** 쉽게

12 _____ 이른 — **early** 일찍

13 **high** 높은 — _____ 높게

14 **lucky** 운 좋은 — _____ 운 좋게

15 **busy** 바쁜 — _____ 바쁘게

16 **good** 훌륭한 — _____ 잘

Step 1 · Check Up 2

다음 문장에서 부사를 찾아 동그라미하고 빈칸에 뜻을 쓰세요.

clerk 점원
answer 대답하다
volleyball 배구

1 I am so hungry. _____

2 The horse runs fast. _____

3 The teacher is very kind. _____

4 We arrive late. _____

5 This drama is really interesting. _____

6 The students study hard. _____

7 He speaks Korean well. _____

8 The room is too dark. _____

9 I am rich enough. _____

10 The car is pretty expensive. _____

11 My grandfather gets up early. _____

12 The cook works busily. _____

13 My father drives carefully. _____

14 The clerk answers kindly. _____

15 The boy passes the exam easily. _____

16 The volleyball player jumps high. _____

다음 괄호 안에서 알맞은 말을 골라 동그라미 하세요.

1 The man smiles (happily, happy).

2 The baby eats soup (slowly, slow).

3 Fatty food is (dangerously, dangerous).

4 They are very (good, well) athletes.

5 The child goes to school (late, lately).

6 The woman swims (fast, fastly).

7 My father is very (angry, angrily).

8 The cat jumps down (quick, quickly).

9 We love her (beautiful, beautifully) paintings.

10 He finds a nice restaurant (easy, easily).

11 The man speaks English (good, well).

12 He is a (kind, kindly) nurse.

13 The pitcher pitches (perfect, perfectly).

14 We have (heavily, heavy) snow in winter.

15 He sings a song (quietly, quiet).

16 Laura studies (hardly, hard).

fatty 기름진
athlete 운동선수
pitch 던지다
perfect 완벽한
hardly
거의 ~하지 않다

부사 · **139**

다음 괄호 안의 말을 알맞은 형태로 고쳐 문장을 완성하세요.

flood 홍수
bark 짖다
loud 시끄러운
through ~을 통해서
tunnel 터널

1 She goes to bed _____. (early)

2 My mother drives _____. (safe)

3 The students solve the quiz _____. (easy)

4 We listen _____. (careful)

5 Jane and Tony work very _____. (hard)

6 Flood is very _____. (dangerous)

7 He plays baseball very _____. (good)

8 He wins the game _____. (perfect)

9 They walk _____. (quiet)

10 All the teachers are too _____. (busy)

11 The dog barks _____. (loud)

12 The basketball player jumps _____. (high)

13 The old man smiles _____. (happy)

14 Jennifer is very _____. (angry)

15 We pass through the tunnel _____. (slow)

16 The girl is a _____ dancer. (good)

Check Up 5

다음 문장에서 빈도부사의 알맞은 위치를 고르세요.

comb 빗질하다
ready 준비된
will ～할 것이다
can ～할 수 있다

1 My son ① goes ② to ③ school ④ early. (always)

2 I ① wash ② my hair ③ once ④ a day. (usually)

3 She ① is ② late ③ for ④ school. (rarely)

4 He ① will ② sing ③ a song ④ in front of people. (never)

5 The girl ① combs ② her ③ hair ④. (often)

6 My mom ① makes ② chocolate ③ cake ④. (sometimes)

7 The boy ① asks ② questions ③ during ④ class. (often)

8 She ① can ② use ③ the ④ chopsticks. (never)

9 My mother ① comes ② home ③ late ④. (sometimes)

10 My ① son ② is ③ happy ④. (always)

11 My family ① goes ② to ③ the zoo ④. (often)

12 I ① can ② enjoy ③ movies ④ at home. (always)

13 They ① visit ② their ③ grandparents ④. (often)

14 You ① are ② ready ③ for ④ class. (rarely)

15 She ① needs ② his ③ help ④. (sometimes)

16 My father ① gets up ② early ③ in the morning ④. (always)

다음 문장의 빈칸에 알맞은 빈도부사를 쓰세요.

shorts 반바지
backpack 배낭
kindness 친절

1 My father and I _____ go camping.

우리 아버지와 나는 캠핑을 자주 간다.

2 His stories are _____ exciting.

그의 이야기들은 보통 흥미진진하다.

3 Tim _____ wears shorts.

팀은 반바지를 가끔 입는다.

4 We can _____ win the game.

우리는 그 경기를 결코 이길 수 없다.

5 Her backpack is _____ heavy.

그녀의 배낭은 항상 무겁다.

6 The student _____ asks questions.

그 학생은 질문을 자주 한다.

7 I can _____ forget his kindness.

나는 결코 그의 친절을 잊을 수 없다.

8 She _____ sees a doctor with her mother.

그녀는 보통 엄마와 함께 의사의 진료를 받는다

9 The mailman is _____ very diligent.

그 우편배달부는 항상 아주 부지런하다.

10 My parents _____ walk to the market.

나의 부모님은 걸어서 가끔 시장에 간다.

다음 우리말과 같도록 빈칸에 알맞은 말을 쓰세요.

turtle 거북
move 움직이다
donkey 당나귀

1 My father drives _____ at night.

우리 아버지는 밤에 안전하게 운전하신다.

2 The team wins the game _____.

그 팀은 그 경기를 완벽히 이긴다.

3 She rides the horse very _____.

그녀는 말을 매우 빨리 탄다.

4 The man dances very _____.

그 남자는 춤을 매우 잘 춘다.

5 The students listen _____.

그 학생들은 주의 깊게 듣는다.

6 I always get up _____ in the morning.

나는 항상 아침에 일찍 일어난다.

7 He _____ likes ice cream.

그는 아이스크림을 정말로 좋아한다.

8 Turtles move very _____.

거북들은 매우 천천히 움직인다.

9 Those students study very _____.

저 학생들은 매우 열심히 공부한다.

10 _____, the donkey falls down.

갑자기 당나귀가 넘어진다.

다음 우리말에 해당하는 빈도부사를 넣어 문장을 다시 쓰세요.

1 I drink some apple juice. (항상)

→ _____

2 She will invite Tom. (결코 ~ 않다)

→ _____

3 We swim in the lake. (때때로)

→ _____

4 The reporter is very busy. (항상)

→ _____

5 I will change my hair style. (거의 ~않다)

→ _____

6 My father cleans the house. (자주)

→ _____

7 Mr. White uses his credit card. (보통)

→ _____

8 We enjoy the party. (자주)

→ _____

9 They eat sweet cookies. (가끔씩)

→ _____

10 The river is frozen in winter. (보통)

→ _____

lake 호수
reporter 기자
hair style 머리 모양
credit card 신용카드
frozen 얼어 붙은

다음 주어진 단어들을 이용하여 문장을 완성하세요.

designer 디자이너
cross 건너다
coach 코치

1 he / teaches / us / kindly / very / always

→ _____

2 hard / I / study / for my dream / usually

→ _____

3 often / the designer / a dress / makes / beautifully

→ _____

4 easily / never / she / the exam / finish / will

→ _____

5 pretty / the man / drives / fast / sometimes

→ _____

6 rarely / you / carefully / cross / the street

→ _____

7 swim / well / always / my sister / can

→ _____

8 talks / the coach / to the players / angrily

→ _____

9 heavily / rains / season / it / in this / often

→ _____

10 sometimes / he / speaks / in the library / quietly

→ _____

다음 빈칸에 알맞은 말을 쓰세요.

Ⅰ 부사의 의미와 쓰임

• 부사란, 형용사, 동사, 다른 부사 등을 꾸며 주는 말로 보통 '_____'라는 의미이다.

• 부사가 형용사를 꾸미는 경우, 부사는 보통 _____ 앞에서 쓰인다.

• 부사가 동사를 꾸미는 경우, 부사는 보통 _____ 뒤에서 쓰인다.

• 부사가 _____를 꾸미는 경우, 꾸며주는 부사는 보통 꾸밈을 받는 부사 앞에서 쓰인다.

2 부사의 형태

• 대부분의 부사는 형용사 끝에 _____를 붙인다.

• 「자음+y」로 끝나는 형용사는 -y를 _____로 바꾸고 _____를 붙인다.

• 형용사와 부사의 형태가 같은 _____(빨리, 빠른), _____(일찍, 이른), _____(늦게, 늦은) 등의 부사에 유의한다.

• _____는 형용사로 '단단한', '어려운'의 뜻이고, 부사로는 '열심히'의 뜻이다.

• _____는 형용사로 '예쁜'의 뜻이고, 부사로 '꽤, 아주, 매우'의 뜻이다.

3 빈도 부사

• 얼마나 자주하는지, 빈도나 횟수를 나타내는 부사이다.

• 빈도 부사는 _____, _____ 뒤에, _____ 앞에 위치한다.

• 빈도 부사에는 _____(항상), usually(보통), _____(종종), sometimes(때때로), rarely(거의 ~ 않다), _____(결코 ~ 않다)가 있다.

다음 문장에서 틀린 부분에 밑줄을 긋고 바르게 고쳐 쓰세요.

dolphin 돌고래
brush 닦다
comfortable 편안한
pianist 피아니스트

1   The dolphin jumps highly.   _____

2   The students study hardly.   _____

3   The boy doesn't cry loud.   _____

4   He speaks kind to sick people.   _____

5   David plays soccer good.   _____

6   I brush my teeth careful.   _____

7   She looks at the photo happy.   _____

8   The children watch a movie quiet.   _____

9   This airplane is prettily big.   _____

10 He finishes his project fastly.   _____

11 The train sometimes arrives lately.   _____

12 The sofa is real comfortable.   _____

13 The boy does his homework easy.   _____

14 The pianist plays the piano soft.   _____

15 She sings a song sad.   _____

16 The model walks beautiful.   _____

다음 문장에서 틀린 부분에 밑줄을 긋고 바르게 고쳐 쓰세요.

noisy 시끄러운
fried 튀긴
history 역사
foolish 어리석은

1   The girls sometimes are noisy. _____

2   My mother goes often to the bank. _____

3   He takes never photos. _____

4   The weather usually is hot in the season. _____

5   Tom gets up rarely early in the morning. _____

6   He teaches history very easy. _____

7   He cooks often a fried chicken. _____

8   The cheetah can run always fast. _____

9   Dan and Jim are very famously actors. _____

10 I listen to usually music. _____

11 Cathy and you work never hard. _____

12 She rides often her bicycle. _____

13 My mother drives the car careful. _____

14 She really plays the game good. _____

15 They swim rarely in the river. _____

16 The men sometimes are foolish. _____

다음 괄호 안의 단어를 참고하여 우리말과 같도록 문장을 완성하세요.

wig 가발
take a walk 산책하다
spaghetti 스파게티
go out 외출하다

1 나는 학교에서 보통 점심을 먹는다. (usually, lunch, have)

→ I _____ at school.

2 나의 엄마는 거의 커피를 마시지 않는다. (coffee, rarely, drink)

→ My mother _____ .

3 그 버스는 가끔 늦게 도착한다. (arrive, sometimes, late)

→ The bus _____ .

4 그는 항상 가발을 쓴다. (always, a wig, wear)

→ He _____ .

5 나는 종종 저녁에 산책을 한다. (a walk, often, take)

→ I _____ in the evening.

6 그는 결코 거짓말을 하지 않는다. (a lie, never, tell)

→ He _____ .

7 그녀는 자주 행복하게 미소 짓는다. (happily, often, smile)

→ She _____ .

8 그는 스파게티를 때때로 요리한다. (sometimes, spaghetti, cook)

→ He _____ .

9 Kate는 항상 한국어를 열심히 공부한다. (study, hard, Korean)

→ Kate _____ .

10 나는 10시 이후에는 결코 나가지 않는다. (go out, never)

→ I _____ after ten.

1 다음 중 부사를 고르세요.

① sad   ② busy

③ slow   ④ carefully

[2~3] 다음 중 형용사와 부사가 잘못 짝지어진 것을 고르세요.

2 ① kind – kindly   ② slow – slowly

③ loud – loudly   ④ early – earlily

3 ① good – well   ② heavy – heavily

③ bad – bad   ④ quick – quickly

4 다음 두 단어의 관계가 나머지와 다른 것은?

① safe – safely

② angry – angrily

③ beautiful – beautifully

④ love – lovely

5 다음 중 밑줄 친 단어의 쓰임이 다른 것을 고르세요.

① He goes to bed late.

② My mother walks fast.

③ The class is noisy.

④ The boys sings happily.

[6~7] 다음 문장의 빈칸에 공통으로 알맞은 말을 고르세요.

6

· The girl is very _____.
· The player is _____ tall.

① fast   ② pretty   ③ so   ④ high

7

· The horse is _____.
· The athlete runs _____.

① fast   ② really   ③ very   ④ hard

[8~9] 다음 중 주어진 빈도부사의 위치로 알맞은 것을 고르세요.

8 ① She ② takes ③ a walk ④ in the evening. (never)

9 ① He ② is ③ quiet ④ in the classroom. (always)

10 다음 괄호 안에 주어진 단어들이 바르게 배열된 것을 고르세요.

나는 저녁 식사 후에 보통 TV를 본다.
(watch, usually, I, dinner, TV, after)

① I watch usually TV after dinner.

② I usually watch TV after dinner.

③ I watch TV after dinner usually.

④ I watch usually TV after dinner.

11 다음 우리말과 같도록 빈칸에 알맞은 말을 고르세요.

비행기는 높이 난다.
Airplanes fly _____.

① fast   ② highly

③ high   ④ late

[12~13] 다음 Jimin의 방과 후 일정을 보고 물음에 답하세요.

Mon.	play soccer, take piano lesson
Tue.	take piano lesson, play soccer,
Wed.	take piano lesson, go to the library
Thu.	play soccer, take piano lesson, go to the library
Fri.	play soccer, take piano lesson, visit grandma

12 다음 빈칸에 들어갈 빈도부사로 알맞은 것을 쓰세요.

Jimin _____ takes piano lesson after school.

13 위 시간표에 대한 설명으로 옳지 <u>않은</u> 것을 고르세요.

① Jimin never plays basketball after school.

② Jimin usually plays soccer after school.

③ Jimin sometimes goes to the library after school.

④ Jimin always visits grandmother after school.

14 다음 중 나머지와 <u>다른</u> 것을 고르세요.

① high   ② early

③ hard   ④ heavy

[15~16] 다음 밑줄 친 부분이 <u>잘못된</u> 문장을 고르세요.

15 ① She <u>always</u> gets up early.

② She <u>never</u> is angry with her friends.

③ She <u>often</u> plays tennis after school.

④ She <u>usually</u> goes to bed late.

16 ① This doll is <u>so</u> pretty.

② My sister swims <u>well</u>.

③ He studies <u>very</u> hard.

④ The teacher speaks <u>loud</u>.

17 다음 빈칸에 들어갈 말로 알맞지 <u>않은</u> 것을 고르세요.

The woman is _____.

① tall   ② late

③ angrily   ④ beautiful

[18~19] 주어진 단어들을 사용하여 다음 문장을 완성하세요.

18 My mother _____ juice in the morning. (drink, usually)

19 Tony _____ you. (often, will, call)

20 다음 문장에서 틀린 부분을 바르게 고쳐 문장을 다시 쓰세요.

The students read books quiet.

→ _____

A 다음 Ann이 일어난 시간표를 보고 사실이면 T, 거짓이면 F를 쓰세요.

	Mon.	Tue.	Wed.	Thu.	Fri.	Sat.	Sun.
Time	7:30	7:10	7:30	7:30	7:30	7:30	10:00

1 Ann usually gets up at 7:30 in the morning.　　　　　(　)

2 Ann never gets up late in the morning.　　　　　(　)

3 Ann gets up late on Sunday.　　　　　(　)

4 Ann always gets up at the same time.　　　　　(　)

5 Ann never gets up at eight o'clock.　　　　　(　)

B 다음 그림을 묘사하는 글을 완성하세요.

John and Bill play basketball.

1 Bill runs _____. (빨리)

2 John jumps _____. (높이)

3 John wins the game _____. (완벽하게)

Unit 8

현재진행형

현재진행형의 의미와 쓰임을 이해할 수 있다.

현재진행형의 부정문과 의문문을 만드는 법을 알고 활용할 수 있다.

진행형을 쓸 수 없는 동사의 종류를 알 수 있다.

진행시제는 어떤 일이 일어나고 있는 중임을 나타내는 시제예요. 현재진행형은 지금 어떤 일이 진행 중임을 나타내요. 지금 하고 있는 일을 표현하며 '~하는 중이다, ~하고 있다'의 뜻을 나타내요. 「be동사(am, are, is) + 동사원형-ing」의 형태로 써요.

Unit 8

현재진행형

1. 현재진행형 문장의 의미와 형태

지금 하고 있는 일을 표현할 때 현재진행형을 사용하며, '~하는 중이다', '~하고 있다'의 뜻으로 be동사(am, are, is)+동사의 -ing의 형태로 쓴다.

현재진행형	be동사(am, are, is)+동사의 -ing 형태	~하는 중이다, ~하고 있다

I am reading a book. 나는 지금 책을 읽고 있다.

My mother is cooking breakfast. 나의 어머니는 아침을 요리하고 있다.

• 동사원형 -ing 형태를 만드는 법

만드는 법		예
대부분 동사	+ing	drink – drinking study – studying
e로 끝나는 동사	e를 없애고 ing를 붙인다.	live – living drive – driving
「단모음(1모음)+ 단자음(1자음)」으로 끝나는 동사	마지막 자음을 하나 더 붙이고 +ing	begin – beginning run – running sit – sitting
-ie로 끝나는 동사	ie를 y로 고치고 +ing	die – dying lie – lying

2. 현재진행형의 부정문

부정문은 be동사의 부정문을 만드는 법과 같은데, be동사(am, are, is) 뒤에 not을 붙여서 부정문을 만든다.

형태	be동사＋not＋동사 -ing형	~하고 있지 않다

I am not watching TV. 나는 TV를 보고 있지 않다.

You are not listening to music. 너는 음악을 듣고 있지 않다.

She is not driving a car. 그녀는 차를 운전하고 있지 않다.

> **Pop Quiz**
> Ⅰ. 다음 괄호 안에서 알맞은 것을 고르세요.
> ❶ Many birds are (fly, flying) in the sky.
> ❷ I am not (wait, waiting) for Judy.

3. 현재진행형의 의문문

의문문은 be동사의 의문문을 만드는 방법과 같은데, be동사(am, are, is)를 주어 앞으로 보내고 문장 끝에 물음표(?)를 붙여서 의문문을 만든다. 대답은 Yes/No와 be동사를 사용한다.

형태	be동사＋주어＋동사 -ing형 ~?	~하고 있니?

You are doing your homework. 너는 너의 숙제를 하고 있다.

→ Are you doing your homework? 너는 너의 숙제를 하고 있니?

　– Yes, I am. / No, I am not. 응, 그래. / 아니, 그렇지 않아.

She is sleeping on the bed. 그녀는 침대에서 자고 있다.

→ Is she sleeping on the bed? 그녀는 침대에서 자고 있니?

　– Yes, she is. / No, she isn't. 응, 그래. / 아니, 그렇지 않아.

4. 진행형으로 사용할 수 없는 동사

진행형은 행동이 일어나고 있는 경우에 쓰기 때문에 소유나 상태를 나타내는 동사는 진행형을 쓰지 않는다.

감정, 상태	감각	소유	인지
like 좋아하다 hate 싫어하다 love 사랑하다 want 원하다	hear 듣다 feel 느끼다 see 보다 taste 맛보다	belong 소유하다 have 가지다	believe 믿다 know 알다 forget 잊다 understand 이해하다

I love you. 나는 너를 사랑한다. I am loving you. (×)

She understands the question.

그녀는 그 질문을 이해하고 있다.

> have는 '먹다', '시간을 보내다'의 경우에는 진행형이 가능하다.

I am having lunch now. (○) 나는 지금 점심을 먹고 있다.

We are having a good time. (○) 우리는 즐거운 시간을 보내고 있다.

They are having books. (×) → have 그들은 책들을 가지고 있다.

He is having a cold. (×) → has 그는 감기에 걸려 있다.(걸렸다)

Pop Quiz

2. 다음 대화 중 괄호 안에서 알맞은 것을 고르세요.

❶ A: Are you (write, writing) a diary?

　　B: Yes, I am.

❷ A: (Is, Are) he studying English?

　　B: No, he (isn't, aren't).

다음 동사의 -ing형을 골라 동그라미 하세요.

1 walk (walkking, walking)

2 hit (hiting, hitting)

3 smile (smileing, smiling)

4 come (coming, comeing)

5 stop (stopping, stoping)

6 bring (bringing, bring)

7 carry (carriing, carrying)

8 have (haveing, having)

9 look (looking, lookking)

10 read (reading, readding)

11 play (plaiing, playing)

12 go (going, gooing)

13 dance (dancing, danceing)

14 cut (cutting, cuting)

15 plan (planing, planning)

16 talk (talking, talkking)

17 put (puting, putting)

18 paint (painting, paintting)

19 stay (staying, staing)

20 help (helping, helpping)

21 drop (dropping, droping)

22 drive (driveing, driving)

23 work (workking, working)

24 give (giveing, giving)

25 open (openning, opening)

26 buy (buying, buiing)

27 listen (listening, listenning)

28 live (living, liveing)

29 visit (visiting, visitting)

30 eat (eating, eatting)

다음 빈칸에 동사의 -ing형을 쓰세요.

1	come	_____	2	listen	_____
3	cook	_____	4	build	_____
5	play	_____	6	cut	_____
7	carry	_____	8	jump	_____
9	begin	_____	10	fall	_____
11	read	_____	12	study	_____
13	plan	_____	14	bring	_____
15	die	_____	16	write	_____
17	eat	_____	18	sleep	_____
19	ride	_____	20	send	_____
21	walk	_____	22	climb	_____
23	run	_____	24	make	_____
25	take	_____	26	buy	_____
27	dance	_____	28	drink	_____
29	lie	_____	30	say	_____

다음 괄호 안에서 알맞은 것을 골라 동그라미 하세요.

lie 거짓말하다
past 과거
die 죽다

1   She (is helping, helping) the young child.

2   Many people (are walking, are walk) on the street.

3   Mr. Brown (is getting, getting) on the bus.

4   Lucy and you (are having, is having) dinner.

5   The woman is (lieing, lying) about her past.

6   My sister (taking, is taking) a shower.

7   Dan (is carrying, is carring) his laptop.

8   The child (is draw, is drawing) a picture.

9   She and he (are enjoying, is enjoying) the party.

10 He (is buying, is buy) some flowers for his wife.

11 The boy is (do, doing) his homework now.

12 My sister (is staying, is stays) in New York.

13 Jessica (is calling, are calling) her mother.

14 The fish (are dying, is dieing) under the river.

15 He (is making, is makeing) some cookies.

16 The children (are flying, are fliing) the kites.

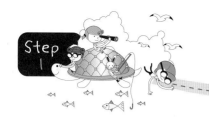

다음 문장에서 밑줄 친 부분의 우리말 뜻을 빈칸에 쓰세요.

boots 부츠		
twice 두 번		
fix 고치다		
hug 껴안다		

1 Paul <u>watches TV</u> after dinner.　　＿＿＿＿＿＿＿

He is <u>watching TV</u> now.　　＿＿＿＿＿＿＿

2 Susie <u>wears boots</u>.　　＿＿＿＿＿＿＿

She is <u>wearing boots</u> now.　　＿＿＿＿＿＿＿

3 They <u>play soccer</u> on Sundays.　　＿＿＿＿＿＿＿

They <u>are playing soccer</u> now.　　＿＿＿＿＿＿＿

4 My mom <u>swims</u> twice a week.　　＿＿＿＿＿＿＿

She is <u>swimming</u> now.　　＿＿＿＿＿＿＿

5 Mr. Yoon <u>teaches English</u>.　　＿＿＿＿＿＿＿

Mr. Yoon is <u>teaching English</u> now.　　＿＿＿＿＿＿＿

6 I <u>keep a diary</u> every day.　　＿＿＿＿＿＿＿

I am <u>keeping a diary</u> now.　　＿＿＿＿＿＿＿

7 My aunt <u>bakes bread</u> on Friday.　　＿＿＿＿＿＿＿

She is <u>baking bread</u> now.　　＿＿＿＿＿＿＿

8 The man <u>fixes chairs</u>.　　＿＿＿＿＿＿＿

He is <u>fixing chairs</u> now.　　＿＿＿＿＿＿＿

9 Mr. Harrel <u>hugs his son</u>.　　＿＿＿＿＿＿＿

He is <u>hugging his son</u> now.　　＿＿＿＿＿＿＿

10 He <u>rides a bicycle</u> on weekend.　　＿＿＿＿＿＿＿

He is <u>riding a bicycle</u> now.　　＿＿＿＿＿＿＿

다음 동사를 이용하여 현재진행형 문장을 완성하세요.

cell phone 휴대폰
speech 연설
knock 노크하다

1 He _____ dinner. (have)

2 We _____ TV now. (watch)

3 Judy _____ her homework. (do)

4 He _____ his room. (clean)

5 They _____ on the playground. (run)

6 I _____ a song. (sing)

7 The man _____ high. (jump)

8 You _____ English now. (study)

9 The baby _____ loudly. (cry)

10 You _____ a book there. (read)

11 The woman _____ her cell phone. (use)

12 John _____ on a chair. (sit)

13 Mr. and Mrs. White _____ home. (come)

14 She _____ the violin in the concert. (play)

15 My mother _____ her speech. (begin)

16 A man _____ on the door. (knock)

다음 괄호 안에서 알맞은 것을 골라 동그라미 하세요.

1 He (is loving, loves) his wife.

2 Many people (are knowing, know) the news.

3 Mr. Brown (is hearing, hears) someone's voice.

4 My mom (is having, has) a cold.

5 The woman (is brushing, brush) her hair.

6 I (am using, uses) the front door.

7 Dan (is understanding, understands) her mind.

8 It (is tasting, tastes) sweet.

9 He and you (like, are liking) each other.

10 My brother (is climbing, climb) the mountain.

11 The girls (has, are having) lunch.

12 My sister (is believing, believes) the story.

13 Lisa (needs, is needing) sunglasses.

14 The umbrella (is belonging, belongs) to Joshua.

15 She (is hating, hates) hot food.

16 Jimmy (is having, has) a small house.

someone 누군가
brush 빗질하다
climb 오르다
mind 마음
each other 서로
belong ~에 속하다

다음 문장을 현재진행형 문장으로 바꾸어 쓰세요.

1 The foreigner studies Korean.

→ _____

2 Alice lies about the accident.

→ _____

3 My brother looks for the key.

→ _____

4 It snows a lot.

→ _____

5 The turtles move slowly.

→ _____

6 She drinks some water.

→ _____

7 I eat a lot of cookies.

→ _____

8 They visit an old place.

→ _____

9 The girl chats with her friends.

→ _____

10 The woman knit a scarf in the room.

→ _____

foreigner 외국인
look for ~을 찾다
chat 수다를 떨다
knit 뜨개질하다

다음 주어진 말을 사용하여 현재진행형 부정문이나 의문문을 완성하세요.

lie 눕다, 거짓말하다
feed 먹이를 주다
machine 기계
jump rope
줄넘기하다

1 I _____ _____ _____ to music. (listen)

2 They _____ _____ the road. (cross)

3 John _____ _____ to the students. (lie)

4 The fat dog _____ _____ fast. (run)

5 They _____ _____ for a post office. (look)

6 Mike _____ _____ his cat. (feed)

7 They _____ _____ this new machine. (use)

8 The girls and boys _____ _____ rope. (jump)

9 _____ you _____ an elephant? (draw)

10 _____ he _____ any snack? (bring)

11 _____ you _____ dinner? (have)

12 _____ the student _____ his homework? (do)

13 _____ Jack _____ the computer well? (fix)

14 _____ they _____ the chairs? (move)

15 _____ Emma _____ now? (laugh)

16 _____ Amy _____ books there? (read)

Build Up 3

다음 문장을 지시대로 바꾸어 쓰세요. 의문문의 경우 대답도 완성하세요. (부정문은 축약형을 쓸 것)

set 세우다, 치다
hard 심하게
boil 끓이다, 삶다

1 You are setting the tent.
(의문문) _____ – Yes, _____
(부정문) _____

2 They are helping the sick.
(의문문) _____ – Yes, _____
(부정문) _____

3 It is raining hard now.
(의문문) _____ – No, _____
(부정문) _____

4 She is smiling at me.
(의문문) _____ – No, _____
(부정문) _____

5 People are walking on the street.
(의문문) _____ – Yes, _____
(부정문) _____

6 Mr. White is sleeping now.
(의문문) _____ – Yes, _____
(부정문) _____

7 My mother is boiling water.
(의문문) _____ – No, _____
(부정문) _____

8 They are writing letters.
(의문문) _____ – Yes, _____
(부정문) _____

다음 빈칸에 알맞은 말을 쓰세요.

1 현재진행형은 지금 하고 있는 일을 표현하는 말로, '~하는 중이다', '_____'는 뜻이다. _____ +
동사의 _____형으로 쓰며, 주어에 따라 be동사의 형태가 **am, are, is**로 바뀐다.

2 동사의 –ing형 만들기

만드는 법		예
대부분의 동사	+ing	_____ – drinking _____ – studying
e로 끝나는 동사	_____를 없애고 ing를 붙인다.	live – _____ drive – _____
「단모음(1모음)+ 단자음(1자음)」으로 끝나는 동사	마지막 _____을 하나 더 붙이고 +ing	begin – _____ run – _____ sit – _____
_____로 끝나는 동사	ie를 _____로 고치고 +ing	die – _____ lie – _____

3 현재진행형의 부정문은 _____ 뒤에 _____을 붙여서 만든다. 의문문은 be동사를 _____ 앞으로
보내고 문장 끝에 물음표(?)를 붙여서 만든다. 의문문에 대한 대답은 _____나 No와 be동사를 사용
한다.

4 _____을 나타내는 동사(like, hate, love 등), _____을 나타내는 동사(hear, feel, see 등),
_____를 나타내는 동사(have, belong 등), _____를 나타내는 동사(understand, know 등)
는 진행형을 만들 수 없다.

다음 문장을 지시대로 바꾸고, 의문문의 경우 대답도 완성해 보세요.

highway 고속도로
locked 잠긴

1 You like the singer.

(의문문) _____ – Yes, _____

2 Sumi is playing the piano.

(부정문) _____

3 They closes the store early.

(부정문) _____

4 The girls are skating on the ice.

(의문문) _____ – Yes, _____

5 Matt is swimming in the lake?

(의문문) _____ – No, _____

6 The bus goes fast on the highway.

(의문문) _____ – Yes, _____

7 My mother is baking cookies.

(부정문) _____

8 The door is locked.

(부정문) _____

9 The movie begins at seven o'clock.

(의문문) _____ – No, _____

10 Tom is sitting on the bench.

(의문문) _____ – Yes, _____

다음 문장에서 틀린 부분에 밑줄을 긋고, 바르게 고쳐 쓰세요.

future 미래
grass 풀
sound 소리

1 He thinking about his future.   → _____

그는 미래에 대해 생각 중이다.

2 She is needing a pencil   → _____

그녀는 연필이 필요하다.

3 They are have lunch on the grass. → _____

그들은 풀밭 위에서 점심을 먹고 있다.

4 Does Mr. White misses his family? → _____

White씨는 그의 가족을 그리워합니까?

5 Jessy is listen to the radio.   → _____

Jessy는 라디오를 듣는 중이다.

6 They are stay in Paris.   → _____

그들은 파리에서 머물고 있다.

7 Sue is having a blue skirt.   → _____

Sue는 파란색 치마를 가지고 있다.

8 They are hearing strange sound.   → _____

그들은 이상한 소리를 듣는다.

9 He is understanding the question. → _____

그는 그 질문을 이해하고 있다.

10 My mother calling my father.   → _____

나의 엄마는 아빠에게 전화하는 중이다.

다음 〈보기〉의 단어를 이용하여 문장을 완성하세요. 필요하면 형태를 바꿔 쓰세요.

taxi 택시

| 〈보기〉 | take | eat | keep | swim |
| | drive | buy | know | listen |

1 그들은 아이스크림을 먹고 있니?

→ _____ ice cream?

2 우리 엄마는 그 상점에서 사과를 사신다.

→ _____ at the store.

3 Minho는 음악을 듣고 있지 않다.

→ Minho _____ to music.

4 그녀는 지금 일기를 쓰고 있다.

→ _____ a diary now.

5 그는 지금 택시를 운전하고 있니?

→ _____ now?

6 Sumin과 나는 사진을 찍고 있지 않다.

→ Sumin and I _____ a picture.

7 그 어린 소년은 수영장에서 수영을 한다.

→ The little boy _____ .

8 너는 내 이름을 알고 있다.

→ _____ my name.

1 다음 빈칸에 공통으로 들어갈 말로 알맞은 것을 고르세요.

> · Tom's sister _____ helping her mother.
> · Eric _____ having dinner.

① are   ② is

③ doing   ④ being

[2~3] 다음 중 동사원형과 -ing 형태가 바르게 짝지어진 것을 고르세요.

2 ① come – comeing
② teach – teaching
③ run – runing
④ sit – siting

3 ① fix – fixxing
② eat – eatting
③ cut – cutting
④ write – writeing

4 다음 우리말을 영어로 쓸 때, 빈칸에 알맞은 것을 고르세요.

> 수진은 지금 우리에게 거짓말하고 있다.
> Sujin is _____ to us now.

① lie   ② lies

③ lyeing   ④ lying

[5~6] 다음 대화의 빈칸에 알맞은 것을 고르세요.

5
> A: Is he sleeping in his room?
> B: _____

① He is.   ② No, he isn't.
③ He isn't.   ④ Yes, he does.

6
> A: _____ they riding bikes?
> B: Yes, they _____.

① Is   ② Are
③ Do   ④ Be

7 다음 중 짝지어진 대화가 <u>어색한</u> 것을 고르세요.

① A: Are they studying?
  B: Yes, they are.
② A: Is Sarah dancing?
  B: No, she isn't.
③ A: Are you crying?
  B: No, you aren't.
④ A: Is he running?
  B: Yes, he is.

[8~13] 다음 문장을 지시대로 바꾸어 쓰세요.

8 She takes a picture of her dog.
(현재진행형)

→ _____

9 Jessica is sitting on a bench. (현재형)

→ _____

10 He is drawing his family. (의문문)

→ _____

11 James is reading a book in the bookstore. (의문문)

→ _____

12 They are chatting with their friends. (부정문)

→ _____

13 She sells chocolate cookies. (부정문)

→ _____

[14~15] 다음 문장 중 올바른 것을 고르세요.

14 ① I is listening to the radio.
② The dogs is running fast.
③ My brother is taking a shower.
④ They are skateing on the ice.

15 ① We are liking her.
② Joshua is hating sour food.
③ She is hearing strange voice.
④ Mrs. Kim is having breakfast.

16 다음 빈칸에 알맞은 것을 고르세요.

> They are swimming in the pool _____.

① yesterday   ② tomorrow
③ last night   ④ now

[17~18] 다음 의문문에 대한 대답을 완성하세요.

17 A: Are you driving a car now?
B: Yes, _____ _____.

18 A: Are the children doing their homework?
B: Yes, _____ _____.

[19~20] 주어진 단어를 활용해 문장을 완성하세요.

19 그녀는 그의 컴퓨터를 사용하고 있다. (use)
→ She _____ his computer.

20 그 물고기들이 지금 죽어가고 있다. (die)
→ The fish _____ now.

서술형 평가

A 다음 그림을 보고, 그림을 묘사하는 글을 완성하세요.

There are many people in the park. The man _____ a sandwich. The girl _____ with her dog. The woman is holding a baby. The baby _____ sadly. The old woman _____ on the bench. The boy _____ a bicycle.

B 다음 질문에 대한 대답을 영어로 쓰세요.

1 Are you studying English now?
  – _____

2 Do you know your grandmother's name?
  – _____

3 Is your mother working now?
  – _____

4 Does your teacher teach kindly?
  – _____

172 · Unit 8

1 다음 주어진 단어의 관계와 같도록 빈칸에 알맞은 것을 고르세요.

old: young   safe: _____

① easy   ② dangerous
③ difficult   ④ poor

2 다음 문장을 부정문으로 바르게 바꾼 것을 고르세요.

There is a key on the table.

① There not is a key on the table.
② There not a key on the table.
③ There isn't a key on the table.
④ There aren't a key on the table.

3 다음 중 빈칸에 들어갈 말로 올바르지 않은 것을 고르세요.

Mr. Lee is a _____ teacher.

① very   ② kind
③ diligent   ④ handsome

4 다음 문장에서 **틀린** 부분을 찾아 바르게 고쳐 쓰세요.

Many tomato are in the basket.

_____ → _____

5 다음 문장 중 바른 것을 고르세요.

① This is very a old house.
② It is new my cell phone.
③ These are famous two pictures.
④ They are very smart girls.

6 다음 대화의 빈칸에 알맞은 말을 쓰세요.

A: Is it hot?
B: No, it isn't. It's _____. (따뜻해)

_____

7 빈칸에 들어갈 말로 알맞은 것을 고르세요.

I have some _____.

① cake   ② eraser
③ ball   ④ book

8 다음 중 밑줄 친 부분의 쓰임이 **잘못된** 것을 고르세요.

① Do they have <u>any</u> food?
② He doesn't eat <u>some</u> cookies.
③ I meet <u>some</u> friends.
④ Do you ask <u>any</u> questions?

[9~10] 다음을 읽고, 물음에 답하세요.

John ⓐ_____ at seven o'clock. He washes his face and hair in the morning. He has breakfast every day. He ⓑ_____ to school on foot. He comes home at five o'clock. He has dinner with his family. He watches often TV after dinner. He usually goes to bed at ten.

9 윗글의 빈칸 ⓐ, ⓑ에 들어갈 말이 순서대로 바르게 짝지어진 것을 고르세요.

① get up – come
② wake up – go
③ gets up – comes
④ wakes up – goes

10 윗글의 밑줄 친 문장에서 틀린 부분을 고쳐 다시 쓰세요.

→ _____

11 다음 밑줄 친 부분 중 바르지 않은 것을 고르세요.

① Jim <u>washes</u> his face.
② He <u>likes</u> oranges.
③ My boy <u>smiles</u> at me.
④ My sisters <u>loves</u> the painting.

12 다음 문장 중 올바른 것을 고르세요.

① He doesn't takes a picture.
② Jane doesn't call her mother.
③ My son doesn't drinks coffee.
④ They don't walks to school.

13 다음 빈칸에 들어갈 말이 순서대로 올바르게 짝지어진 것을 고르세요.

Tom: What are you doing?
Jenny: I'm making some cake.
Tom: Oh, I like cake.
        What are you mixing?
Jenny: A little _____, a few
        _____, and a little _____.

① butter – eggs – milk
② butter – sugar – eggs
③ eggs – butter – milk
④ sugar – water – butter

14 다음 대화의 빈칸에 들어갈 말이 순서대로 바르게 짝지어진 것을 고르세요.

A: _____ your sisters
   play computer games?
B: Yes, _____.

① Do – they do
② Is – she is
③ Does – she does
④ Are – they are

15 다음 빈칸에 알맞은 말을 쓰세요.

· Ann speaks English. And she speaks French, _____.
· I don't eat lemons. And my father doesn't eat lemons, _____.

_____, _____

16 다음 빈칸에 들어갈 말로 알맞은 것을 고르세요.

She doesn't sell much _____.

① sugar   ② flowers
③ carrots   ④ bananas

17 다음 중 정도에 따른 빈도부사가 올바른 순서로 배열된 것을 고르세요.
① always > never > sometimes > rarely > usually > often
② often > always > usually > rarely > sometimes > never
③ always > usually > sometimes > often > rarely > never
④ never > usually > rarely > sometimes > always > often

18 다음 질문에 대한 대답으로 알맞은 것을 고르세요.

A: Is Sally having dinner?
B: _____

① Yes, she is.
② Yes, she does.
③ No, she doesn't.
④ No, she wasn't.

19 다음 중 밑줄 친 부분의 쓰임이 바른 것을 고르세요.
① It is tasting sour.
② I am needing a new jacket.
③ She is wanting cold water.
④ He is cooking spaghetti.

20 다음 현재시제를 현재진행형으로 바꾼 문장에서, 틀린 부분을 바르게 고쳐 쓰세요.

Mr. and Mrs. Kim drink some tea.
→ Mr. and Mrs. Kim drinking some tea.

_____ → _____

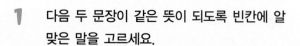
1 다음 두 문장이 같은 뜻이 되도록 빈칸에 알맞은 말을 고르세요.

> There are four children in the room.
> = Four children _____ in the room.

① is   ② are

③ aren't   ④ isn't

2 다음 주어진 단어의 관계와 같도록 빈칸에 알맞은 말을 고르세요.

> kind: kindly → happy: _____

① happiness   ② unhappy

③ happily   ④ unhappiness

3 다음 중 동사의 3인칭 단수형이 바르지 <u>않은</u> 것을 고르세요.

① watchs   ② goes

③ plays   ④ looks

4 다음 문장 중 바르지 <u>않은</u> 것을 고르세요.

① There is five benches in the park.

② There isn't an apple in the box.

③ There are some fish in the tank.

④ There are two buses on the road.

[5~6] 다음을 읽고, 물음에 답하세요.

> _____
> Elephant are big. Three giraffes are tall. Four monkeys are on the tree. They are eating bananas. There is a sheep. A man is beside the sheep.

5 윗글의 빈칸에 들어갈 말로 알맞은 것을 고르세요.

① In the zoo are many animals.

② In the zoo is many animals.

③ There are many animals in the zoo.

④ Many animals there are in the zoo.

6 다음 질문에 알맞은 답을 고르세요.

> Are the monkey eating bananas?

① Yes, it is.

② No, it isnt.

③ Yes, they are.

④ No, they aren't.

7 다음 빈칸에 들어갈 말로 바르지 <u>않은</u> 것을 고르세요.

> _____ watch a movie on TV.

① My friends   ② Brian

③ She and I   ④ They

다음 빈칸에 들어갈 말이 순서대로 바르게 짝지어진 것을 고르세요.

8

> · Joshua usually _____ homework alone.
> · She and her friend sometimes _____ homework together.

① do – do   ② do – does

③ does – do   ④ does – does

9

> · We _____ a car.
> · She _____ English.

① drive – study

② drive – studies

③ drives – study

④ drives – studies

10 다음 빈칸 @~ⓒ에 들어갈 말이 순서대로 바르게 짝지어진 것을 고르세요.

> A: ___@___ your mother bake cookies?
> B: No, she ___ⓑ___ . She ___ⓒ___ some bread.

        @   ⓑ   ⓒ

① Do   – doesn't – bake

② Does – doesn't – gives

③ Does – does   – give

④ Do   – does   – gives

11 다음 빈칸에 공통으로 들어갈 말을 쓰세요.

> · There are _____ castles in the farm.
> · Would you like _____ water?

_____

12 다음 문장을 부정문으로 만들 때, not이 들어갈 위치를 고르세요.

We ① are ② carrying ③ some ④ chairs.

13 다음 문장에서 틀린 부분을 올바르게 고쳐 쓰세요.

> Does John and she listen to music?

_____ → _____

14 다음 밑줄 친 말을 대신할 수 있는 말을 쓰세요.

> There are <u>many</u> books in the box.

_____

15 다음 중 동사원형과 -ing형이 바르지 <u>않은</u> 것을 고르세요.

① meet – meeting
② eat – eating
③ drive – driving
④ lie – lieing

16 다음 중 빈도부사의 위치가 바르지 <u>않은</u> 것을 고르세요.

① He often forgets telephone numbers.
② She always smiles.
③ It's often very cold in winter.
④ He cleans never his room.

17 다음 빈칸에 들어갈 말로 알맞은 것을 고르세요.

> She drives a car _____ .

① slow   ② beautiful
③ carefully   ④ difficult

18 다음 문장의 뜻을 우리말로 쓰세요.

> I have few photos.

_____

19 다음 〈보기〉와 같이 형용사의 부사형을 쓰세요.

> 〈보기〉 angry - angrily

(1) fast   – _____
(2) good – _____

20 다음 Kathy의 방과 후 일정을 보고 빈칸에 알맞은 빈도부사를 쓰세요.

Mon.	read books, study English
Tue.	study English, read books
Wed.	study English, play computer games
Thu.	read books, study English, play computer games
Fri.	read books, study English, visit grandparents

Kathy _____ study English after school.

초등 영어 교재의 베스트셀러

초등 영어 문법 실력 쌓기!

Grammar Builder

2

Answer Key

Answer Key

 Unit 1 일반동사의 현재시제

Pop Quiz

1. ❶ read ❷ drinks
2. ❶ likes ❷ go

■ Step 1 ┃ Check Up 1   p. 17

1. sing 2. watch 3. does 4. cleans 5. drink
6. has 7. jumps 8. stay 9. cries 10. read
11. turns 12. sits 13. come 14. plays 15. works
16. snows

■ Step 1 ┃ Check Up 2   p. 18

1. helps 2. walk 3. gets 4. have 5. eats
6. know 7. carries 8. goes 9. enjoy 10. buys
11. finish 12. stays 13. sees 14. pass 15. makes
16. study

■ Step 1 ┃ Check Up 3   p. 19

1. My dad 2. They 3. She 4. Tom 5. Jim
6. Paul 7. He 8. They 9. Jim and Alex 10. We
11. My uncle 12. She 13. It 14. You
15. He and she 16. Ann

■ Step 1 ┃ Check Up 4   p. 20

1. They 2. His friend 3. Mike and John
4. My dad 5. The scientists 6. They 7. We
8. He 9. The woman 10. She 11. A year

12. She 13. The babies 14. You and I 15. I
16. Jessica

■ Step 1 ┃ Check Up 5   p. 21

1. watches 2. flies 3. sings 4. has 5. sit
6. look 7. wears 8. invite 9. drives 10. sleeps
11. run 12. play 13. makes 14. waits 15. comes
16. know

■ Step 1 ┃ Check Up 6   p. 22

1. carries 2. work 3. rains 4. meets 5. helps
6. walk 7. has 8. likes 9. does 10. goes
11. drink 12. writes 13. sleeps 14. hurries
15. watches 16. buy

■ Step 2 ┃ Build Up 1   p. 23

1. makes 2. plays 3. close 4. washes 5. cross
6. enjoy 7. buys 8. ends 9. begins 10. carry
11. cleans 12. has 13. pays 14. fixes 15. read
16. passes

■ Step 2 ┃ Build Up 2   p. 24

1. plays tennis once a week.
2. visit London every year.
3. enjoys delicious food. 4. miss the family.
5. flies well. 6. studies in the library.
7. has a blue hat. 8. catch balls well.
9. brushes the kid's hair everyday.
10. cook in the morning.

1. The boys know them.
2. The children run to the park.
3. The girl wears glasses.
4. They have two daughters.
5. The baby eats something all day.
6. The hunter looks for deer.
7. The stars shine in the sky.
8. Suji watches TV after lunch.
9. My parents sell clothes at the market.
10. He catches five mosquitoes.

■ **Step 3** ǀ Jump 1   p. 26

1. 행동, 상태, 행동, 상태   2. 3인칭 단수, 동사원형
3. s, es, comes, washes, does, i, says, has

■ **Step 3** ǀ Jump 2   p. 27

1. goes 2. studies 3. plays 4. buys 5. misses
6. has 7. cries 8. watches 9. flies 10. washes
11. finishes 12. teaches 13. carries 14. fixes
15. does 16. kisses

■ **Step 3** ǀ Jump 3   p. 28

1. She has a beautiful dress.
2. The kid plays with his friends.
3. The birds sit in the tree.
4. Mr. Brown works at a bank.
5. They swim in the river.
6. The boys play basketball after school.
7. He and she drink milk every morning.
8. John and I meet her at the bus stop.
9. My sister writes a postcard.
10. The children ride bikes in the park.

■ **Step 3** ǀ Jump 4   p. 29

1. The kids have a smart phone.

2. They study science.
3. My brother always copies me.
4. The cat catches fish very well.
5. They enjoy the party.
6. My sister does yoga everyday.
7. Those girls buy apples there.
8. This boy carries the boxes.
9. The children go to the playground.
10. The woman watches a movie every weekend.

■ **Step 4** ǀ 실전 평가   p. 30

1. ④ 2. ② 3. ③ 4. ③ 5. ① 6. rides 7. do
8. ③ 9. ④ 10. ③ 11. ④ 12. have 13. makes
14. ③ 15. ④ 16. ③ 17. ④ 18. ①
19. look at the pictures. 20. fixes the computer.

1. study의 3인칭 단수형은 y를 i로 바꾸고 -es를 붙여서 만든다.
2. have의 3인칭 단수형은 불규칙 변화로 has이다.
3. -sh로 끝나는 동사의 3인칭 단수형은 -es를 붙여서 만든다.
4. 동사가 teaches로 3인칭 단수형인 것으로 보아 주어에는 3인칭 단수 주어가 와야 한다.
5. 동사가 동사원형이 왔으므로 주어에는 3인칭 단수형을 제외한 주어가 올 수 있다.
6. 주어가 3인칭 단수 주어임으로 3인칭 단수형 동사가 와야 한다.
7. 주어가 복수형이므로 동사에는 동사원형이 와야 한다.
8. 주어가 3인칭 단수이면, 동사는 3인칭 단수형이 와야 한다.
16. 주어에 명사가 올 경우, 명사 주어는 3인칭으로 단수, 복수에 따라 동사를 맞게 써야 한다.

■ **Step 5** ǀ 서술형 평가   p. 32

A 1. studies 2. has 3. likes
B 1. wash, have[eat], do, have[eat], watch, go

2. washes, has[eats], goes, has[eats], studies, goes

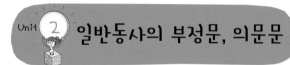

Unit 2 일반동사의 부정문, 의문문

Pop Quiz

1. ❶ don't ❷ doesn't
2. ❶ Do ❷ live

■ Step 1 I Check Up 1   p. 37

1. don't 2. doesn't 3. doesn't 4. don't
5. doesn't 6. don't 7. doesn't 8. don't
9. doesn't 10. doesn't 11. don't 12. don't
13. doesn't 14. don't 15. doesn't 16. don't

■ Step 1 I Check Up 2   p. 38

1. Do, meet 2. Does, arrive 3. Does, do
4. Do, drive 5. Do, look 6. Does, sing
7. Do, read 8. Do, have 9. Does, live
10. Does, fly 11. Does, choose 12. Do, start
13. Does, come 14. Do, pay 15. Does, stand
16. Does, like

■ Step 1 I Check Up 3   p. 39

1. too 2. either 3. either 4. either 5. too 6. too
7. either 8. too 9. either 10. too

■ Step 1 I Check Up 4   p. 40

1. don't, tell 2. Does, enter 3. doesn't, belong

---

4. doesn't, start 5. Does, look 6. don't, ride
7. doesn't, ask 8. Do, chat 9. Does, clean
10. don't, meet

■ Step 1 I Check Up 5   p. 41

1. Do you come early?
2. Does he play the piano?
3. She doesn't look at the sky.
4. Do they meet at the bus stop?
5. Jenny doesn't miss the train.
6. Does it rain in London?
7. I don't remember his phone number.
8. Does Jane do her homework?

■ Step 1 I Check Up 6   p. 42

1. Yes, he does. 2. No, she doesn't.
3. No, she doesn't. 4. Yes, I(we) do.
5. No, she doesn't. 6. Yes, you do.
7. No, he doesn't. 8. Yes, it does.
9. Yes, they do. 10. Yes, she does.
11. No, they don't. 12. No, he doesn't.
13. Yes, they do. 14. Yes, he does.
15. No, they don't. 16. Yes, she does.

■ Step 2 I Build Up 1   p. 43

1. Do you know, You don't know
2. Does she speak, She doesn't speak
3. Do they drink, They don't drink
4. Does Emily get, Emily doesn't get
5. Do they use, They don't use
6. Does the taxi stop, The taxi doesn't stop
7. Does Sarah buy, Sarah doesn't buy
8. Do the girls wear, The girls don't wear

■ Step 2 I Build Up 2   p. 44

1. either 2. too 3. too 4. either 5. too 6. too
7. either 8. either 9. too 10. either

1. I don't take a piano lesson every day.

2. Does Peter stay home alone?, he doesn't.

3. Tom and Tony don't have many friends.

4. She doesn't her homework.

5. Does the concert start on time?, it does.

6. Do the kids swim in the pool?, they don't.

7. Does the man take a shower?, he does.

8. The woman doesn't cross the street.

9. Does Judy call her mother?, she doesn't.

10. Do you hear my voice?, I(We) don't.

1. 일반동사, don't, doesn't, don't, doesn't, don't

2. 주어, Do, Does, 물음표, 동사원형, Yes, No, 1, you, you, we, we, we, we, doesn't

3. too, either

1. Do you have   2. Paul doesn't listen to

3. Does she wear   4. Do they go   5. That isn't

6. My son doesn't remember   7. Are you

8. Does John call   9. My friend doesn't ride

10. Do you use   11. They don't laugh

12. Is he   13. Does the party begin

14. Do your sisters live   15. Henry doesn't arrive

16. The books aren't

1. Do they come from China?, they do.

2. Does Mr. Brown write letters?, he doesn't.

3. We don't go to school on Sundays.

4. She doesn't know Mr. Park.

5. Do you do the dishes after meals?, I(we) do.

6. Mr. Baker isn't a cook.

7. Does your daughter have a doll?, she doesn't.

8. Your grandmother doesn't read a book.

9. Does Suji keep a diary every day?, she does.

10. Are these your photos?, they are

1. Does   2. doesn't enter   3. Does he play

4. Do   5. don't have   6. meet   7. don't wait

8. Do you worry   9. he doesn't   10. doesn't see

11. travel   12. Do   13. either   14. Does your sister

15. doesn't wash   16. doesn't ring

1. ① 2. ④ 3. ④ 4. ③ 5. ② 6. ③ 7. ③ 8. ①

9. ③ 10. ② 11. ④

12. Do the students wear school uniforms?

13. ④ 14. ④ 15. ③

16. Your friends don't study at the library., Do your friends study at the library?

17. exercises, Does Henry exercise every day?

18. aren't, They don't arrive at school.

19. Does the party begin

20. She doesn't do

1. 일반동사가 있는 문장의 부정문은 do(es)n't를 붙여서 만드는데, 그 위치는 일반동사 앞에 위치한다.

2. 일반동사가 있는 문장의 부정문을 만들 때, 주어가 3인 칭 단수일 때는 doesn't를 사용해서 나타낸다.

4. 일반동사가 있는 문장의 부정문을 만들 때, 주어가 복 수일 때는 don't를 사용해서 나타낸다.

5. win이라는 일반동사가 있으므로 aren't가 아니고 don't 를 써야 한다.

6. 일반동사의 의문문의 문장 앞에 Do(es)를 붙이고 동사 는 주어가 3인칭 단수일지라도 동사원형을 쓴다.

7. 일반동사가 있는 문장의 의문문을 만들 때, 주어가 3인 칭 단수이면 Does를 사용해서 나타낸다.

8. 일반동사가 있는 문장의 의문문에 대한 대답은 Yes나 No를 사용하여 나타내며 do나 does를 이용하여 나타 낸다.

9. 일반동사가 있는 문장의 의문문에 대한 대답에서 주어가 3인칭 단수이면 does를 이용하여 나타낸다.

10. 주어가 복수 명사이므로 do를 이용하여 나타낸다.

11. 문장에서 주어를 먼저 찾아보면 쉽게 답을 찾을 수 있는데, ④번의 경우에는 동사가 없으므로 be동사가 들어간다는 것을 알 수 있다.

13. '~도, 또한'이라는 뜻을 가진 말은 too와 either인데 too는 긍정문에 사용하고 either는 부정문에 사용한다.

■ Step 5 | 서술형 평가   p. 52

A He, loves, doesn't, cook, are, don't, watch, don't, either, don't, have

B Do, don't, Does

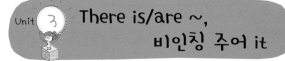
Unit 3 There is/are ~, 비인칭 주어 it

Pop Quiz

1. ❶ is ❷ are
2. ❶ It ❷ It

■ Step 1 | Check Up 1   p. 57

1. is 2. are 3. is 4. is 5. are 6. is 7. is 8. are 9. is 10. is 11. are 12. are 13. is 14. are 15. is 16. are

■ Step 1 | Check Up 2   p. 58

1. There is 2. There are 3. There is 4. There is

5. There are 6. There are 7. There is 8. There is 9. There are 10. There is 11. There are 12. There is 13. There is 14. There are 15. There are 16. There is

■ Step 1 | Check Up 3   p. 59

1. It 2. It 3. It 4. It 5. It 6. There 7. It 8. It 9. It 10. It

■ Step 1 | Check Up 4   p. 60

1. a lady 2. pictures 3. a bunch of flowers 4. 7 days 5. a park 6. a kitten 7. a lot of snow 8. an ant 9. Mr. and Mrs. White 10. five Mondays 11. some sugar 12. a moon 13. many fish 14. a little flour 15. 12 months 16. a cute puppy

■ Step 1 | Check Up 5   p. 61

1. Are there, There are not[aren't]
2. Is there, There is not[isn't]
3. Are there, There are not[aren't]
4. Is there, There is not[isn't]
5. Are there, There are not[aren't]
6. Are there, There are not[aren't]
7. Are there, There are not[aren't]
8. Is there, There is not[isn't]

■ Step 1 | Check Up 6   p. 62

1. there are, there aren't 2. there are, there aren't
3. there are, there aren't 4. there is, there isn't
5. there are, there aren't 6. there is, there isn't
7. there is, there isn't 8. there are, there aren't

■ Step 2 | Build Up 1   p. 63

1. There is 2. There are 3. There are
4. There is 5. There are 6. There is

7. There are 8. There is 9. There is

10. There are 11. There is 12. There are

13. There is 14. There are 15. There are

16. There is

■ Step 2 ı Build Up 2   p. 64

1. There are 2. It is 3. It takes 4. It is

5. There is 6. There is 7. It is 8. There are

9. It is 10. There is

■ Step 2 ı Build Up 3   p. 65

1. Is there a soccer team in the city?, There is
   not[isn't] a soccer team in the city.

2. Are there bees on the flowers?, There are
   not[aren't] bees on the flowers.

3. Is there a lot of flour in the paper bag?, There
   is not[isn't] a lot of flour in the paper bag.

4. Is there little rice in the plastic bag?, There is
   not[isn't] little rice in the plastic bag.

5. Are there foreign teachers in this school?,
   There are not[aren't] foreign teachers in this
   school.

6. Are there a lot of people in the gym?, There
   are not[aren't] a lot of people in the gym.

7. Are there few kittens in the pet shop?, There
   are not[aren't] few kittens in the pet shop.

8. Is there a library between the bank and the
   hospital?, There is not[isn't] a library between
   the bank and the hospital.

■ Step 3 ı Jump 1   p. 66

1. be동사, 셀 수 없는, is, are 2. not
3. there, 물음표, Yes, No 4. It, 그것, it

■ Step 3 ı Jump 2   p. 67

1. There is a chair beside the sofa.

2. There are Tom and his sister in the classroom.

3. There is a white table in my house.

4. There are many rivers in Korea.

5. There is a bank behind the building.

6. There are six pieces of pizza on the table.

7. There are some oranges in the basket.

8. There is a small fox in the cage.

9. There are three bottles of juice on the shelf.

10. There is a lot of cheese in the storage.

■ Step 3 ı Jump 3   p. 68

1. There is a little milk in the glass.

2. There are four Chinese restaurants in this town.

3. Are there many people in the park?

4. There aren't difficult problems in the exam.

5. There is one man in the gym.

6. There is not a lot of rain in summer.

7. There are five bunches of grapes in the basket.

8. Take an umbrella. It is raining.

9. Is there some pepper in the jar?

10. There are four pieces of furniture in the room.

■ Step 3 ı Jump 4   p. 69

1. There are many plants at the flower shop.

2. Are there many fish under the sea?, there are.

3. Is there some paper on the desk?, there isn't.

4. It takes two hours to Jeju island.

5. There is not some flour in the paper bag.

6. Are there a lot of people in the office?, there
   aren't.

7. There are four seasons in Korea.

8. Are there three math classes in a week?, there
   are.

9. Get up. It is nine o'clock now.

10. Are there some old women in the museum?,
    there are.

1. ① 2. ④ 3. ③ 4. ③ 5. ④ 6. ② 7. ③ 8. ②

9. ② 10. ③

11. There is not a bank next to the library.

12. Is there a bus stop around here? 13. ④

14. ① 15. ②

16. Are there three cups of coffee on the table?

17. ② 18. ③

19. There are some singers on the stage.

20. Hurry up. It is 11 o'clock.

1. There is 다음에는 단수 명사가 온다.

2. There are 다음에는 복수 명사가 온다.

4. There is 의문문은 There와 is의 자리를 바꾸고 문장 끝에 물음표(?) 붙여서 만들며 대답은 Yes, No를 이용 하여 there is(긍정) 또는 there isn't(부정)로 나타낸 다.

5. Are there ~?로 물어볼 때는 Yes, No를 이용하여 there are(긍정) 또는 there aren't(부정)로 나타낸다.

6. There is 부정문은 be동사 뒤에 not을 붙여서 나타낸 다.

7. 셀 수 없는 명사인 물질명사는 단수 취급한다.

8. problems라는 복수 명사가 온 것으로 보아 be동사 are가 와야 한다.

10. 시간, 날짜, 요일, 날씨, 명암, 거리 등을 나타낼 주어 로 it을 사용하는 이때의 주어를 비인칭 주어 it이라고 한다.

13. '~이 있다'라는 뜻으로 나타낼 때는 There is/are를 사용하여 나타낸다.

14. sugar는 물질명사로 수량 형용사와 함께 사용하거나 수량을 나타낼 때는 단위를 통해서 나타낸다.

A There are, It, There are, They, four, There is, not

B there isn't, Is, Yes, there is

Unit 4 형용사

1. ❶ handsome ❷ snowy

2. ❶ pretty ❷ green

1. old 2. small 3. short 4. dirty 5. poor

6. strong 7. hungry 8. cold 9. slow 10. short

11. closed 12. busy 13. difficult 14. cheap

15. dry 16. heavy

1. handsome, 잘생긴 2. cool, 멋진 3. great, 훌륭한

4. sleepy, 졸린 5. famous, 유명한 6. big, 큰

7. two, 둘의 8. old, 오래된 9. difficult, 어려운

10. busy, 바쁜 11. blue, 파란색의

12. delicious, 맛있는 13. windy, 바람이 부는

14. lovely, 사랑스런 15. wet, 젖은 16. heavy, 무거운

1. She is a new student.

2. The boy has a very cute puppy.

3. These are their new books.

4. He brings us very happy news.

5. The boys look at these many flowers.

6. Mrs. White is a very kind teacher.

7. It is a very long coat.

8. The three brown leaves are falling.

9. He is a very strong man.

10. I love her beautiful paintings.

1. her yellow skirt 2. many old houses

3. cold water   4. your very nice car

5. a very kind nurse   6. my new umbrella

7. her smart son   8. very useful books

9. That diligent woman   10. an expensive chair

■ Step 1 ｜ Check Up 5   p. 81

1. is high   2. is lazy   3. am cold   4. are red

5. is open   6. are dirty   7. is closed   8. is free

9. are difficult   10. is deep   11. is blue   12. is big

13. is black   14. are pretty[beautiful]   15. is heavy

16. is cute

■ Step 1 ｜ Check Up 6   p. 82

1. My father is very happy.

2. She has a very small dog.

3. Jim is a good baseball player.

4. I like this white sofa.

5. Those are very old houses.

6. The actor is very famous.

7. It is a very useful dictionary.

8. These are very clean sneakers.

9. These dirty glasses are hers.

10. My brother has two small bicycles.

■ Step 2 ｜ Build Up 1   p. 83

1. is clean   2. is not[isn't] dry

3. are not[aren't] weak   4. is not[isn't] cheap

5. is safe   6. is not[isn't] thin

7. is not[isn't] diligent   8. are not[aren't] short

9. is not[isn't] wide   10. are not[aren't] slow

■ Step 2 ｜ Build Up 2   p. 84

1. Anna is not[isn't] hungry.

2. Mr. Baker is not[isn't] poor.

3. My teacher is not[isn't] old.

4. The lake is not[isn't] dirty.

5. It is not[isn't] hot today.

6. The house is not[isn't] small.

7. The furniture is not[isn't] light.

8. It is not[isn't] light here.

9. The nurse is not[isn't] unkind.

10. The street is not[isn't] safe.

■ Step 2 ｜ Build Up 3   p. 85

1. These bags are heavy.

2. That little boy is smart.

3. Those horses are very fast.

4. The water is not[isn't] cold.

5. She is diligent and kind.

6. My father is thin and tall.

7. My brother and I are hungry.

8. This swimming suit is wet.

9. The window is open.

10. These pictures are great.

■ Step 3 ｜ Jump 1   p. 86

1. 명사, ~한, 지시, 성질   2. 한정적, 주어, 동사, 서술적

3. 형용사, 명사, 부사, 형용사, 소유격, 수량, 성질

■ Step 3 ｜ Jump 2   p. 87

1. long dress.

2. pretty girls.

3. These are very interesting books.

4. This is a very clean bottle.

5. That is a beautiful park.

6. This is a famous singer.

7. This is a very small jacket.

8. This is a yellow sweater.

9. This is a very expensive watch.

10. Those are very big elephants.

■ Step 3 ｜ Jump 3   p. 88

1. She is a busy girl.   2. Those balls aren't big.

3. That is a very hungry bear.

4. They are smart students.

5. These roofs are green.

6. I live in this old big house.

7. Jake is a very excellent cook.

8. My father is very angry.

9. Jim and Olivia are very famous actors.

10. Those are five new televisions.

■ **Step 3** ㅣ Jump 4   p. 89

1. very busy player.

2. She has a very pretty dog.

3. That is his white car.

4. Jake is a very kind teacher.

5. That is an expensive house.

6. It is very hot water.

7. This is a very new dictionary.

8. They are their pink hats.

9. Those are very beautiful places.

10. Those are sweet cookies.

■ **Step 4** ㅣ 실전 평가   p. 90

> 1. ④ 2. ③ 3. ③ 4. ② 5. ④ 6. ② 7. ④ 8. ①
> 9. My red box is heavy.
> 10. My father is a very brave and kind police
>   officer.
> 11. These many white flowers are in the park.
> 12. ① 13. ④ 14. ③ 15. ① 16. ④ 17. short, fat
> 18. dangerous, dirty
> 19. These computers are very expensive.
> 20. He is a very wise boy.

1. easy의 반대말은 difficult이고, clean의 반대말은 dirty이다.

2. hot의 반대말은 cold이다.

3. 형용사는 명사 바로 앞에 와서 명사를 꾸며 주는 역할을 하는데, 이 문장에서 형용사는 interesting이다.

4. 문장에 and가 있는 것으로 보아 동일한 역할을 하는

것이 2개가 나오는 것을 알 수 있는데, 여기서는 expensive와 old가 형용사로 명사를 꾸미는 역할을 한다.

5. 지시형용사의 경우 this, that이 있는데, 복수형 문장일 때는 these, those를 사용하여 나타낸다.

7. 소유격이나 지시형용사와 명사가 함께 올 경우, 관사 (a/an, the)는 붙이지 않는다.

8. 형용사가 명사를 꾸며 주는 경우 위치가 정해져 있는 데, a/an+부사+형용사+명사 또는 소유격+형용사+명사로 쓴다.

12. 보통 명사에 –ly를 붙여 형용사를 만들 수 있다.

14. 형용사는 명사 바로 앞에 와서 명사를 꾸며 주는데, 이를 형용사의 '한정적 용법'이라고 한다. 또한 형용사가 동사 뒤에 와서 주어의 성격을 나타내기도 하는데, 이를 형용사의 '서술적 용법'이라고 한다.

■ **Step 5** ㅣ 서술형 평가   p. 92

> A ❶ driver, is, careful ❷ movie, is, interesting
> B green, tall, red, black, big

Unit **5**   **Some, Any, All, Every**

Pop Quiz

1. ❶ some ❷ any

2. ❶ boys ❷ boy

■ **Step 1** ㅣ Check Up 1   p. 96

1. some 2. any 3. some 4. any 5. any 6. any

7. any 8. any 9. some 10. any 11. some

12. some 13. any 14. some 15. any 16. some

1. some 2. carrots 3. balls 4. any 5. any
6. food 7. information 8. pets 9. any 10. some
11. sugar 12. dresses 13. any 14. some
15. some 16. any

■ Step 1 | Check Up 3   p. 98

1. every 2. All 3. All 4. every 5. all 6. every
7. every 8. Every 9. All 10. Every 11. All
12. every 13. All 14. every 15. Every 16. every

■ Step 1 | Check Up 4   p. 99

1. needs 2. like 3. is 4. are 5. wants 6. eat
7. are 8. passes 9. play 10. has 11. love
12. are 13. wants 14. like 15. are 16. policeman

■ Step 1 | Check Up 5   p. 100

1. any 2. any 3. some 4. any 5. any 6. any
7. some 8. any 9. any 10. some 11. any
12. any 13. some 14. any 15. some 16. some

■ Step 1 | Check Up 6   p. 101

1. every 2. every 3. All 4. All 5. Every 6. All
7. All 8. All 9. Every 10. Every 11. every
12. every 13. every 14. all 15. all 16. Every

■ Step 2 | Build Up 1   p. 102

1. Would you like some coffee?
2. They don't have any fresh milk.
3. She sells some beautiful red roses.
4. Does she cut any tall trees?
5. His daughters want some cute cats.
6. I don't eat any hot soup.
7. We carry some heavy boxes.
8. Do you have any red T-shirts?
9. We don't have any long coats.

10. Some brown leaves are falling.

■ Step 2 | Build Up 2   p. 103

1. Does Joe raise any pets?, Joe doesn't raise
   any pets.
2. Does your friend eat any cookies?, Your friend
   doesn't eat any cookies.
3. Does he write any poems?, He doesn't write
   any poems.
4. Does her father help any poor people?, Her
   father doesn't help any poor people.
5. Do they visit any kids everyday?, They don't
   visit any kids everyday.
6. Does he sell any vegetables?, He doesn't sell
   any vegetables.
7. Does she teach any young students?, She
   doesn't teach any young students.

■ Step 2 | Build Up 3   p. 104

1. Every student doesn't go to school.
2. Do you have any friends?
3. All children play outside.
4. Would you like some orange juice?
5. We play soccer every Friday.
6. We send some e-mails to mom.
7. All girls like the handsome singer.
8. Every winter vacation I visit my uncle.

■ Step 3 | Jump 1   p. 105

1. 몇몇의, 긍정문, 의문문, 셀 수 있는, 셀 수 없는, 복수,
   some, 요청, some, some, some, any, 의문문,
   any, any
2. 모든, 단수, 3, 단수, is, 복수, are

■ Step 3 | Jump 2   p. 106

1. friend, friends 2. some, any 3. some, any
4. any, some 5. some, any 6. any, some

7. any, some 8. some, any 9. coffees, coffee
10. some, any 11. tree, trees 12. some, any
13. any, some 14. any, some 15. flours, flour
16. word, words

■ **Step 3 |** Jump 3   p. 107

1. all, every 2. every, all 3. All, Every
4. every, all 5. All, Every 6. Every, All
7. All, Every 8. all, every 9. Every, All
10. every, all 11. every, all 12. all, every
13. all, every 14. all, every 15. every, all
16. all, every

■ **Step 3 |** Jump 4   p. 108

1. see some friends.
2. go to church every Sunday?
3. want some bread? 4. have any questions.
5. All students arrive 6. have some food?
7. find any information.
8. Every one waits for him.
9. Every hope comes true.
10. All children like the teacher.

■ **Step 4 |** 실전 평가   p. 109

1. ③ 2. ① 3. ③ 4. ④ 5. ④ 6. ② 7. some
8. any 9. ③ 10. ② 11. Do you want some cake?
12. All students arrive on time.
13. Do you have any questions?
14. All information is useful to him.
15. ③ 16. ② 17. ② 18. ③
19. My family goes camping every weekend.
20. Do all snakes have poison?

1. some이나 any 뒤에는 셀 수 있는 명사와 셀 수 없는
   명사 모두 올 수 있다. 셀 수 없는 명사는 복수 형태로
   쓸 수 없다.
2. every 다음에는 반드시 단수명사가 오며, 단수로 취급

한다.
3. 긍정문에는 some을, 부정문과 의문문에는 any를 쓴
   다.
4. all 다음에는 반드시 복수명사가 오며, 복수로 취급한
   다.
5. 긍정문에는 some을 사용하지만, 부정문에는 any를
   써야 한다.
6. 긍정문에는 some을 사용하지만, 의문문에는 any를
   써야 한다.
9. all+복수명사 뒤에 일반동사가 올 경우, -s나 -es가
   붙지 않은 동사원형이 온다.
10. every+단수명사 뒤에 be동사가 올 경우, 단수 형태
    인 is가 온다.
15. 요청하는 경우에는 의문문일지라도 some을 쓴다.

■ **Step 5 |** 서술형 평가   p. 112

A 1. Some 2. any 3. Every 4. Some
B any, some, any, Every

Unit 6 수량형용사

Pop Quiz

1. ❶ many ❷ much
2. ❶ a little ❷ few

1. many 2. much 3. Many 4. Many 5. much
6. many 7. much 8. many 9. Many 10. many
11. many 12. much 13. many 14. Many
15. Much 16. many

1. a lot of 2. much 3. a lot of 4. a lot of
5. many 6. much 7. much 8. a lot of 9. a lot of
10. much 11. much 12. a lot of 13. a lot of
14. much 15. a lot of 16. a lot of

1. a few 2. a little 3. a few 4. a little 5. little
6. a little 7. few 8. little 9. a few 10. few
11. few 12. little 13. a little 14. few 15. a little
16. few

1. toys 2. flowers 3. snow 4. work 5. oil
6. chairs 7. money 8. clothes 9. shampoo
10. comic books 11. bread 12. ideas 13. names
14. tea 15. water 16. cookies

1. a few 2. a little 3. A few 4. Little 5. few
6. a little 7. little 8. a few 9. little 10. a little

1. a little 2. a few 3. many 4. much 5. a few
6. much 7. Many 8. few 9. A few 10. little

1. a lot of 2. many, a lot of 3. a lot of, many
4. much, a lot of 5. a lot of 6. much, a lot of
7. a lot of, many 8. many, a lot of
9. much, a lot of 10. many, a lot of
11. a lot of 12. many, a lot of 13. Many, A lot of
14. much, a lot of 15. a lot of

1. little 2. a few 3. little 4. few 5. a little
6. a few 7. a little 8. A few 9. Little 10. few

1. A little chocolate 2. many[a lot of] mountains
3. little homework 4. a little flour
5. much[a lot of] food 6. a few dolls
7. Few letters 8. little cheese
9. Many[A lot of] restaurants
10. much[a lot of] information

1. 많은, 셀 수 있는, 셀 수 없는, a lot of, 의문문, 부정문
2. 약간의, 거의 없는, 셀 수 있는, 셀 수 없는, a few, little
3. a few, 복수형, much, little, 복수형

1. much[a lot of] 2. little 3. many
4. much[a lot of] 5. Few 6. a lot of 7. singers
8. few 9. many[a lot of] 10. A few 11. a lot of
12. few 13. a little 14. little 15. Many[A lot of]
16. a little

1. ices, ice 2. a few, a little 3. a little, a few
4. ball, balls 5. much, many 6. pant, pants
7. few, little 8. little, few 9. much, many[a lot of]
10. student, students 11. much, a lot of
12. much, many[a lot of] 13. Much, Many

14. are, is 15. child, children 16. time, times

■ Step 3 | Jump 4   p. 129

1. a few dogs 2. needs a little help

3. read few books 4. He drinks little water

5. Many/A lot of trees 6. Much/A lot of bread

7. speaks little English 8. Jake buys a lot of meat

9. We have many/a lot of holidays

■ Step 4 | 실전 평가   p. 130

1. ④ 2. ③ 3. ③ 4. ② 5. ① 6. ③ 7. a lot of

8. ④ 9. ③ 10. ④ 11. ③ 12. ② 13. ③

14. salts, salt 15. a little, a few[some] 16. ③ 17. ②

18. a little 19. much[a lot of] 20. few

1. many는 셀 수 있는 명사 앞에 쓰여서 수가 많음을 나타낸다.

2. much는 셀 수 없는 명사 앞에 쓰여서 양이 많음을 나타낸다.

3. little은 '거의 없는'이라는 의미로 셀 수 없는 명사 앞에 쓰인다.

4. a lot of는 셀 수 있는 명사와 셀 수 없는 명사 앞에 모두 쓸 수 있으며 수나 양이 많음을 나타낸다.

5. some은 셀 수 있는 명사와 셀 수 없는 명사 앞에 쓰여 '약간의', '몇몇의'라는 뜻으로 쓰인다.

6. a few와 few는 셀 수 있는 명사 앞에 쓰인다.

7. a lot of는 셀 수 있는 명사와 셀 수 없는 명사 앞에 모두 쓸 수 있다.

8. a few와 few는 셀 수 있는 명사 앞에 쓰이고, a little과 little은 셀 수 없는 명사 앞에 쓰인다.

12. meat는 셀 수 없는 명사이므로 much나 a lot of가 와야 한다.

13. time은 셀 수 없는 명사이고 긍정문이기 때문에 올 수 있는 것은 a little과 a lot of이다. 그런데 두 번째 문장에서 countries는 셀 수 있는 명사의 복수형이므로 a few가 들어가야 한다.

16. milk는 셀 수 없는 명사이고 문장이 긍정문이므로 a

lot of를 사용하여 나타내야 한다.

17. a few와 a little은 긍정의 의미로 쓰이고, few와 little은 not 없이 부정의 의미를 나타낸다.

■ Step 5 | 서술형 평가   p. 132

A 1. a lot of 2. a few 3. a little 4. a few 5. Little

B 1. a lot of rain in London

   2. a lot of snow in Toronto

   3. little snow in New York

Unit 7 부사

Pop Quiz

1. ❶ slowly ❷ very

2. ❶ ① ❷ ②

■ Step 1 | Check Up 1   p. 137

1. fast 2. happily 3. late 4. beautifully 5. bad

6. slowly 7. kindly 8. quick 9. quietly

10. carefully 11. easy 12. early 13. high

14. luckily 15. busily 16. well

■ Step 1 | Check Up 2   p. 138

1. so, 아주 2. fast, 빨리 3. very, 매우 4. late, 늦게

5. really, 정말로 6. hard, 열심히 7. well, 잘

8. too, 너무 9. enough, 충분히 10. pretty, 매우

11. early, 일찍 12. busily, 바쁘게

13. carefully, 조심스럽게 14. kindly, 친절하게

15. easily, 쉽게 16. high, 높게

■ Step 1 | Check Up 3

1. happily 2. slowly 3. dangerous 4. good
5. late 6. fast 7. angry 8. quickly 9. beautiful
10. easily 11. well 12. kind 13. perfectly
14. heavy 15. quietly 16. hard

■ Step 1 | Check Up 4 p. 140

1. early 2. safely 3. easily 4. carefully 5. hard
6. dangerous 7. well 8. perfectly 9. quietly
10. busy 11. loudly 12. high 13. happily
14. angry 15. slowly 16. good

■ Step 1 | Check Up 5 p. 141

1. ① 2. ① 3. ② 4. ② 5. ① 6. ① 7. ① 8. ② 9.
① 10. ③ 11. ① 12. ② 13. ① 14. ② 15. ① 16. ①

■ Step 1 | Check Up 6 p. 142

1. often 2. usually 3. sometimes 4. never
5. always 6. often 7. never 8. usually
9. always 10. sometimes

■ Step 2 | Build Up 1 p. 143

1. safely 2. perfectly 3. fast 4. well 5. carefully
6. early 7. really 8. slowly 9. hard
10. Suddenly

■ Step 2 | Build Up 2 p. 144

1. I always drink some apple juice.
2. She will never invite Tom.
3. We sometimes swim in the lake.
4. The reporter is always very busy.
5. I will rarely change my hair style.
6. My father often cleans the house.
7. Mr. White usually uses his credit card.
8. We often enjoy the party.
9. They sometimes eat sweet cookies.

10. The river is usually frozen in winter.

■ Step 2 | Build Up 3 p. 145

1. He always teaches us very kindly.
2. I usually study hard for my dream.
3. The designer often makes a dress beautifully.
4. She will never finish the exam easily.
5. The man sometimes drives pretty fast.
6. You rarely cross the street carefully.
7. My sister can always swim well.
8. The coach talks angrily to the players.
9. It often rains heavily in this season.
10. He sometimes speaks quietly in the library.

■ Step 3 | Jump 1 p. 146

1. ~하게, 형용사, 동사, 부사
2. -ly, -i, -ly, fast, early, late, hard, pretty
3. be동사, 조동사, 일반동사, always, often, never

■ Step 3 | Jump 2 p. 147

1. highly, high 2. hardly, hard 3. loud, loudly
4. kind, kindly 5. good, well 6. careful, carefully
7. happy, happily 8. quiet, quietly
9. prettily, pretty 10. fastly, fast 11. lately, late
12. real, really 13. easy, easily 14. soft, softly
15. sad, sadly 16. beautiful, beautifully

■ Step 3 | Jump 3 p. 148

1. sometimes are, are sometimes
2. goes often, often goes
3. takes never, never takes
4. usually is, is usually
5. gets up rarely, rarely gets up 6. easy, easily
7. cooks often, often cooks
8. run always, always run 9. famously, famous
10. listen to usually, usually listen to
11. work never, never work

12. rides often, often rides 13. careful, carefully

14. good, well 15. swim rarely, rarely swim

16. sometimes are, are sometimes

■ **Step 3** | Jump 4   p. 149

1. usually have lunch 2. rarely dinks coffee

3. sometimes arrives late 4. always wears a wig

5. often take a walk 6. never tells a lie

7. often smiles happily

8. sometimes cooks spaghetti

9. always studies Korean hard

10. never go out

■ **Step 4** | 실전 평가   p. 150

1. ④ 2. ④ 3. ③ 4. ④ 5. ③ 6. ② 7. ① 8. ②

9. ③ 10. ② 11. ③ 12. always 13. ④ 14. ④

15. ② 16. ④ 17. ③ 18. usually drinks

19. will often call

20. The students read books quietly.

1. 부사는 일반적으로 형용사 뒤에 -ly를 붙여서 만든다.

2. early는 형용사와 부사의 형태가 같은 단어이다.

3. bad의 부사는 -ly를 붙여서 만들며 badly이다.

4. 명사에 -ly를 붙이면 형용사가 된다.

5. noise(잡음)라는 명사에 -y가 붙여 noisy(시끄러운) 이라는 형용사가 된 단어이다.

6. pretty는 형용사로는 '예쁜'이라는 뜻이고 부사로는 '매우, 아주'라는 뜻이다.

7. fast는 형용사와 부사의 형태가 같은 단어이다.

8. 빈도부사는 일반동사 앞에 위치한다.

9. 빈도부사는 be동사와 조동사 뒤에 위치한다.

11. high는 형용사와 부사의 형태가 같은 단어이다. highly는 '매우'라는 뜻의 부사이다.

12. 피아노 수업은 매일 있는 것을 할 수 있다.

14. high, early, hard의 공통점은 형용사와 부사의 형태 가 같은 단어들이다.

16. loud는 형용사로 동사 뒤에 들어가기 위해서는 부사

의 형태인 loudly가 되어야 한다.

17. 주어를 보충 설명해 주는 역할을 하는 것은 형용사이 므로 angrily가 아닌 angry가 되어야 한다.

■ **Step 5** | 서술형 평가   p. 152

A 1. T 2. F 3. T 4. F 5. T
B fast, high, perfectly

Unit 8 현재진행형

Pop Quiz

1. ❶ flying ❷ waiting

2. ❶ writing ❷ Is, isn't

■ **Step 1** | Check Up 1   p. 157

1. walking 2. hitting 3. smiling 4. coming

5. stopping 6. bringing 7. carrying 8. having

9. looking 10. reading 11. playing 12. going

13. dancing 14. cutting 15. planning 16. talking

17. putting 18. painting 19. staying 20. helping

21. dropping 22. driving 23. working 24. giving

25. opening 26. buying 27. listening 28. living

29. visiting 30. eating

■ **Step 1** | Check Up 2   p. 158

1. coming 2. listening 3. cooking 4. building

5. playing 6. cutting 7. carrying 8. jumping

9. beginning 10. falling 11. reading 12. studying

13. planning 14. bringing 15. dying 16. writing

17. eating 18. sleeping 19. riding 20. sending
21. walking 22. climbing 23. running
24. making 25. taking 26. buying 27. dancing
28. drinking 29. lying 30. saying

■ Step 1 | Check Up 3　　　　　　　　p. 159

1. is helping 2. are walking 3. is getting
4. are having 5. lying 6. is taking 7. is carrying
8. is drawing 9. are enjoying 10. is buying
11. doing 12. is staying 13. is calling
14. are dying 15. is making 16. are flying

■ Step 1 | Check Up 4　　　　　　　　p. 160

1. TV를 본다 / TV를 보고 있다
2. 부츠를 신는다 / 부츠를 신고 있다
3. 축구를 한다 / 축구를 하고 있다
4. 수영을 한다 / 수영을 하는 중이다
5. 영어를 가르친다 / 영어를 가르치고 있다
6. 일기를 쓴다 / 일기를 쓰고 있다
7. 빵을 굽는다 / 빵을 굽는 중이다
8. 의자들을 고치다 / 의자들을 고치고 있다
9. 그의 아들을 껴안는다 / 그의 아들을 껴안고 있다
10. 자전거를 탄다 / 자전거를 타고 있는 중이다

■ Step 1 | Check Up 5　　　　　　　　p. 161

1. is having 2. are watching 3. is doing
4. is cleaning 5. are running 6. am singing
7. is jumping 8. are studying 9. is crying
10. are reading 11. is using 12. is sitting
13. are coming 14. is playing 15. is beginning
16. is knocking

■ Step 1 | Check Up 6　　　　　　　　p. 162

1. loves 2. know 3. hears 4. has 5. is brushing
6. am using 7. understands 8. tastes 9. like
10. is climbing 11. are having 12. believes
13. needs 14. belongs 15. hates 16. has

■ Step 2 | Build Up 1　　　　　　　　p. 163

1. The foreigner is studying Korean.
2. Alice is lying about the accident.
3. My brother is looking for the key.
4. It is snowing a lot.
5. The turtles are moving slowly.
6. She is drinking some water.
7. I am eating a lot of cookies.
8. They are visiting an old palace.
9. The girl is chatting with her friends.
10. The woman is knitting a scarf in the room.

■ Step 2 | Build Up 2　　　　　　　　p. 164

1. am not listening 2. aren't crossing 3. isn't
lying 4. isn't running 5. aren't looking 6. isn't
feeding 7. aren't using 8. aren't jumping
9. Are, drawing 10. Is, bringing 11. Are, having
12. Is, doing 13. Is, fixing 14. Are, moving
15. Is, laughing 16. Is, reading

■ Step 2 | Build Up 3　　　　　　　　p. 165

1. Are you setting the tent?, I am[We are]. You
   aren't setting the tent.
2. Are they helping the sick?, they are. They
   aren't helping the sick.
3. Is it raining hard now?, it isn't., It isn't raining
   hard now.
4. Is she smiling at me?, she isn't., She isn't
   smiling at me.
5. Are people walking on the street?, they are.,
   People aren't walking on the street.
6. Is Mr. White sleeping now?, he is., Mr. White is
   sleeping now.
7. Is my mother boiling water?, she isn't., My
   mother isn't boiling water.
8. Are they writing letters?, they are., They aren't
   writing letters.

■ Step 3 ┃ Jump 1

1. ~하고 있다, be동사, -ing
2. -ie, e, 자음, y, drink, study, living, driving, beginning, running, sitting, dying, lying
3. be동사, not, 주어, Yes
4. 감정, 감각, 소유, 인지

■ Step 3 ┃ Jump 2 p. 167

1. Do you like the singer?, I do.
2. Sumi is not[isn't] playing the piano.
3. They do not[don't] close the store early.
4. Are the girls skating on the ice?, they are.
5. Is Matt swimming in the late, he isn't.
6. Does the bus go fast on the highway?, it is.
7. My mother is not[isn't] baking cookies.
8. The door isn't locked.
9. Does the movie begin at 7 o'clock?, it doesn't.
10. Is Tom sitting on the bench?, he is.

■ Step 3 ┃ Jump 3 p. 168

1. thinking, is thinking 2. is needing, needs
3. have, having 4. misses, miss
5. listen, listening 6. stay, staying
7. is having, has 8. are hearing, hear
9. is understanding, understands
10. calling, is calling

■ Step 3 ┃ Jump 4 p. 169

1. Are they eating 2. My mother buys apples
3. isn't listening 4. She is keeping
5. Is he driving a taxi 6. aren't taking
7. swims in the pool 8. You know

■ Step 4 ┃ 실전 평가 p. 170

1. ② 2. ② 3. ③ 4. ④ 5. ② 6. ② 7. ③

8. She is taking a picture of her dog.
9. Jessica sits on a bench.
10. Is he drawing his family?
11. Is James reading a book in the bookstore?
12. They are not[aren't] chatting with their friends.
13. She doesn't sell chocolate cookies.
14. ③ 15. ④ 16. ④ 17. I am[we are] 18. they are
19. is using 20. are dying

1. 현재진행형 문장은 be동사(am, are, is)+동사의 -ing형의 형태로 쓴다.
2. 동사의 -ing형은 -e로 끝나는 동사는 e를 없애고 ing를 붙인다. 단모음(1모음) + 단자음(1자음)으로 끝나는 동사는 마지막 자음을 하나 더 붙이고 -ing를 붙인다.
4. -ie로 끝나는 동사는 ie를 y로 고치고 -ing를 붙인다.
5. 현재진행형의 의문문은 be동사의 의문문 만드는 방법과 같은데, be동사(am, are, is)를 주어 앞으로 보내고 문장 끝에 물음표(?)를 붙여서 의문문을 만든다. 대답은 Yes/No와 be동사를 이용한다.
7. you(2인칭)으로 물어보면 대답은 I나 we(1인칭)으로 한다.
12. 현재진행형의 부정문은 be동사의 부정문 만드는 법과 같은데, be동사(am, are, is) 뒤에 not을 붙여서 부정문을 만든다.
15. 진행형은 행동이 일어나고 있는 경우에 쓰기 때문에 감정이나 상태, 소유, 인지를 나타내는 동사들은 진행형을 쓰지 않는다.
16. 현재진행형 문장은 현재 진행되고 있는 일을 나타내므로 과거나 미래를 나타내는 말과는 쓸 수 없다.

■ Step 5 ┃ 서술형 평가 p. 172

A is eating[having], is running, is crying, is sitting, is riding
B 1. Yes, I am[we are]. / No, I am not[we aren't].
   2. Yes, I do[we do]. / No, I don't[we don't].
   3. Yes, she is. / No, she isn't.
   4. Yes, she[he] does. / No, she[he] doesn't.

1. ② 2. ③ 3. ① 4. tomato, tomatoes 5. ④

6. warm 7. ① 8. ② 9. ④

10. He often watches TV after dinner. 11. ④ 12. ②

13. ① 14. ① 15. too, either 16. ① 17. ③ 18. ①

19. ④ 20. drinking, are drinking

1. old와 young은 서로 반대의 뜻을 가진 단어로 safe의 반대의 뜻을 가진 단어는 dangerous이다.

2. There is 구문의 부정문은 be동사 is 다음에 not을 붙이면 된다.

3. 형용사는 명사 앞에서 명사를 꾸며주는 역할을 한다. 형용사가 아닌 단어를 찾으면 된다.

4. many는 '많은'이라는 뜻으로 셀 수 있는 명사의 복수형 앞에서 명사를 꾸며주는 역할을 한다.

5. 형용사는 「소유격＋형용사＋명사」 순서로 쓴다.

7. some은 셀 수 있는 명사와 셀 수 없는 명사 앞에 올 수 있는데, 셀 수 있는 명사는 복수형을 써야 한다.

8. some은 긍정문에 쓰이고, any는 부정문과 의문문에 쓰인다.

9. 주어가 3인칭 단수형일 때 동사는 3인칭 단수형 동사를 써야 한다. 3인칭 단수형 동사는 동사원형에 -s나 -es를 붙여서 만든다.

10. 빈도부사는 일반동사 앞에, be동사와 조동사 앞에 위치한다.

11. 주어가 복수 명사일 때 동사는 동사원형을 쓴다.

12. 일반동사의 부정문은 동사 앞에 don't나 doesn't(주어가 3인칭 단수일 경우)를 붙여서 만든다.

13. little은 셀 수 없는 명사 앞에, few는 셀 수 있는 명사 앞에 쓴다.

14. 일반동사의 의문문은 문장 앞에 Do나 Does(주어가 3인칭 단수일 경우)를 붙이고 동사는 동사원형을 쓰며, 문장 끝에 물음표를 붙인다.

15. '~도, 또한'이라는 뜻의 단어는 too와 either를 사용하여 나타내는데, too는 긍정문에, either는 부정문에 사용한다.

16. '많은'이라는 뜻의 단어는 many와 much가 있는데, many는 셀 수 있는 명사 앞에, much는 셀 수 없는 명사 앞에 쓴다.

18. 현재진행형 문장의 의문문의 대답은 Yes나 No를 사용하여 답하며 주의할 것은 do나 does로 답하는 것이 아닌, be동사를 사용하여 답한다.

1. ② 2. ③ 3. ① 4. ① 5. ③ 6. ③ 7. ② 8. ③

9. ② 10. ② 11. some 12. ② 13. Does, Do

14. a lot of 15. ④ 16. ④ 17. ③

18. 나는 사진이 거의 없다. 19. (1) fast (2) well

20. always

2. 형용사에 -ly를 붙여서 부사를 만들 수 있는데, -y로 끝나는 형용사는 y를 i로 바꾸고 -ly를 붙인다.

3. -ch로 끝나는 동사는 -s가 아닌 -es를 붙여서 만든다.

4. There is/are 구문에서 주어는 be동사 뒤에 오며 주어가 단수이면 There is를 쓰고, 복수이면 There are를 쓴다.

6. 현재진행형 문장의 의문문의 대답은 Yes나 No를 사용하여 답하며 do나 does가 아닌, be동사를 사용한다.

7. 문장의 동사를 보면 동사원형이 온 것을 알 수 있는데, 따라서 주어에 3인칭 단수 주어를 빼고는 모두 올 수 있다.

8. 주어가 3인칭 단수형일 때는 동사는 3인칭 단수형을 써야 하며 3인칭 단수형은 동사원형에 -s나 -es를 붙여서 만든다.

10. 일반동사의 의문문은 문장 앞에 Do나 Does(주어가 3인칭 단수일 경우)를 붙이고 동사는 동사원형을 쓰며, 문장 끝에 물음표를 붙인다.

11. some은 일반적으로 긍정문에 사용하지만 권유나 요청하는 의문문에도 사용할 수 있다.

12. 현재진행형 문장의 부정문은 be동사의 부정문 만드는 방법과 같은데, be동사 뒤에 not을 붙여 주면 된다.

14. many나 much는 a lot of로 바꾸어 쓸 수 있다.

15. 동사의 -ing형을 만들 때 -ie로 끝나는 동사는 -ie를 -y로 바꾸고 -ing를 붙여준다.

16. 빈도부사는 일반동사 앞에, be동사와 조동사 앞에 위치한다.

Memo